PILGRIM'S
PROCESS

PILGRIM'S PROCESS

Essays from the Journey

BRIAN WEST

Fresh Wind Press

PILGRIM'S PROCESS: Essays from the Journey.
Copyright © 2008 by Brian West.

Editorial services provided by: Ed Strauss, inkwell@shaw.ca

Cover design by: Brad Haima, Circle Graphics
www.circle.bc.ca

Interior layout by: Brad Jersak
www.freshwindpress.com

Printed in Canada by D.W. Friesen and Sons, Ltd.

To contact the author: bswest@shaw.ca

ISBN: 978-0-9780174-6-0

Library Archives of Canada information available.

Fresh Wind Press
2170 Maywood Ct.,
Abbotsford, BC
Canada V2S 4Z1
www.freshwindpress.com

DEDICATION

To Sue, my sweetheart of twenty-six years. You have never given up on me and have been a great source of encouragement.

And to my three awesome children who often bring a tear to my eye for good reasons.

CONTENTS

FOREWORD:
BRAD JERSAK

"I am sending you prophets and wise men and teachers." (Jesus in Matt. 23:34)

"Even though you have ten thousand guardians in Christ, you do not have many fathers, for in Christ Jesus I became your father through the gospel." (1Cor. 4:15)

In these days when influential men and women clamor to be recognized as apostles and prophets, establishing their identity through position and title, we the church are in desperate need of the wisdom that comes from intimate fellowship with Christ the Suffering Servant. We need a "word from the Lord" from those whose character has been sculpted by God's heart and by life's journey; whose mantle of ministry marks them as serving fathers and mothers.

This is how I've experienced by friend and mentor, Brian West. At times he's come alongside me as prophet, wise man and teacher. His approach again and again has been that of servant-father in the faith. He has tutored me in stewarding the presence and power of God, ministering inner healing to the extremely broken, and walking with confidence in the realm of spiritual conflict. But even this did not take me into to depths of Brian's heart.

Rather, it was when Brian was being real with me about the raw wounds in his soul, sharing from his guts privately before some renewal meeting where all heaven was about to break loose. And it was when Brian met me in the torments of my own soul and when my only anchor to the reality of Jesus was seeing the kingdom of God in his eyes. He normally treats me as a peer and co-laborer, but it was when he graciously tucked me under his wing and sheltered me from hellish storms that I learned to trust him with my life.

For this reason, I would dearly love you to glean from his wisdom—from God's wisdom in him. The truths herein are life to the soul when all of our triumphalist cliches have turned to plastic.

Brian, thanks for watching my back. I love you.

Brad Jersak
Fresh Wind Christian Fellowship

NOT IN VAIN

God knows.
Tears shed in darkness.
Not in vain.
Time, years, spent on your knees.
Not in vain.
Petitioning our Savior,
for the lost, for the church, for yourself.
Not in vain.
Time spent studying the word of God,
yet still questions.
Not in vain.
Listening to the cries of children.
Listening. Listening. Listening.
Not in vain.
The valley. The winter. The depths of despair,
Not in vain.
Abandoning comfort for an unknown path.
Not in vain.
Rejoicing, delighting, listening.
Not in vain.
God knows,
It was not in vain...

Shelene Mitchell – Listening Prayer Seminar
Peace Community Church, Taylor, BC.

INTRODUCTION: TRUST THE PROCESS

Life is lived one day at time; we are all in the same process. Life is not an event to be endured, but a process of growing and maturing as a human being. I have some good news and some bad news to tell you. The good news is God has a perfect process in mind to bring us to maturity in Christ. The bad news is that God has a perfect process in mind to bring us to maturity in Christ. It seems bad because sometimes it feels like the maturing process is going to kill us. How do we learn to survive and trust that God has this process completely worked out? We need to trust that there is a point to all the trials that we walk through. Do we really know that God is loving and kind or do we just pay lip service to these truths? This book is about learning to trust that God has a process for us to walk through to become mature in our faith.

One of the secrets of this process is to believe and apply the victory that Jesus won on the cross to our lives and let Him live His life though us. We need to learn to enjoy the journey through life. Many of us are destination-oriented: we miss the lessons the journey itself has to teach us as we move through life from goal to goal. Don't get me wrong, goals are important, but not at the sake of experiencing the abundant life that Jesus promised us every day.

I started this process about twenty-seven years ago and God has led me on an incredible journey. I have written a few essays from this journey, and these essays contain stories and lessons learned along the way. I am learning to trust that God knows exactly what we need to mature into our full potential.

I've wanted to write a book ever since I was a little kid. This is my first attempt at such an undertaking. If I would have listened to all the critics around me, I never would have taken the chance and lived out this dream. Life is too short not to live out our dreams, and I encourage you to do so as well. I've heard it said that everyone has at least one book inside him or her waiting to be written. Here is my first attempt, for better or for worse.

I used to be sure about many things; now I have more questions than answers. I used to be a destination person— "Where am I going and how am I going to get there?" I didn't realize that when I gave my life to God, I gave up the right to be in control. As I get older the only thing that I can really control is my attitude. I can make a choice to be joyful or crabby. Jesus is "The Leader" and He calls the shots. His agenda then becomes of primary importance in my life.

There is an interesting Bible verse that I should have memorized from the start. It reads: "For my thoughts are not your thoughts, neither are your ways my ways," declares the LORD. **"As the heavens are higher than the earth, so are my ways higher than your ways and my thoughts than your thoughts"** (Isa. 55: 8, 9).

God is not like us; He's always kind and never goes back on a promise—and apparently the journey of life is just as important as the destination.

As I said, I have wanted to write a book for a long time, but I am better at talking than I am at writing. I am not very disciplined, so it has taken me a long time to even get started. And then there were discouraging thoughts: "Why even try to begin to write? It will never amount to anything." I decided not to listen to that voice; it certainly didn't sound like God to me.

So here I am, wondering what to write. I've been through so many different experiences and circumstances in my life. I've been involved in Christian leadership for about twenty-five years and God has taken me through many interesting seasons. I have just recently come out of a long journey through the desert, a dry time when God had my attention and spoke to me tenderly. I have been finding out how to find water in the midst of dry times.

This verse from the book of Hosea about how God uses

desert seasons comes to mind: **"Therefore I am now going to allure her; I will lead her into the desert and speak tenderly to her."** (Hos. 2:14)

I've come to realize that I am not good at living with a restful attitude in the desert. I want to be somewhere else and I have come to realize that I am a driven person on the inside. I might not appear that way, but that is the truth. Taking time to reflect is not easy for me, but as I do it, I find that it's quite therapeutic. I am becoming a little more contemplative and a little less confused.

I was thinking of calling this book "Things they never taught me in Bible College," but I knew that some people might not appreciate that title. The bulk of my education has been mainly through everyday life. I am very thankful for my Bible College days, but how can a school get you ready to face the trials that you will surely go through in the trenches of everyday living? I never realized how much pastoring takes out of you, but I have a better idea after all these years.

As I write about various experiences that I've had, I do not presume to have arrived; I am still very much in process. That's one of the reasons that I'm taking time to write: I want to share my life with you and I'm finding that it's quite therapeutic to do so. If God can use someone like me then He can certainly use someone like you.

Pastoring seems to be an impossible job when done in my

own strength. I have heard that the average pastor is wounded emotionally once a month and that those wounds take an average of two years to heal. Pastors are either in crisis, just coming through a crisis, or a crisis is looming on the horizon. Who wants to volunteer to answer the call to ministry? This could be a book about leadership principles or maybe it's just the random thoughts of a madman. I'll let you come to your own conclusions. I invite you to take some of these lessons to heart; you never know—your life may be changed as a result!

Here is one of the greatest revelations that I as leader have had lately: "I have needs, and my needs are just as important as everyone else's." Can you imagine the reactions I get when I say this to people? Most understand and laugh with me. Others get this funny look on their face. They can't believe that I would have any needs. I am a leader after all, a dispenser of wisdom and strength, and with little or no resemblance to a human being. But the truth is, leaders are not different than anyone else: we just get good at pretending!

I think that one of the most important jobs of a leader is to point people to the Jesus Christ. We are not to let people feed off of us, but bring them to the Lord. However, when people depend on us to feed them, it can stroke our ego as leaders. When people come to us and need answers for daily life we must point them to the Bible and what Jesus taught.

I think that another important thing is to teach people how to hear the voice of God for themselves rather than telling them what He is saying to them. We have spoon-fed people for far too long, and it has not done them any good. Leaders are to assist people to help them grow and mature in their faith, not just tell them exactly what to do.

I am not setting out to write a book on theology; I want to share some of my experiences to encourage you to keep going rather than giving up. If you think that you have completely blown it or there is no hope for you, just keep reading; this could be the book for you.

I have lived through some very hard times over the last couple of decades. One of my friends put it very well; he asked me during one these difficult times if I could keep breathing. Yes, even if it's dreadfully hard, and all I can do is keep breathing, I know that things are going to get better after a while.

I don't know what you are like, but I'm a very stubborn person. Actually, a lot of people that I have met are quite stubborn. I guess I have to learn the hard way. Almost everyone I know learns this way. I enrolled in the "school of hard knocks" a long time ago, and continue to be a student in this school. Hopefully, I have moved passed grade one in the curriculum. It's a hard way to learn, but once you learn something this way, you won't forget the lessons!

There is a saying that goes something like this: "You won't change until staying the same becomes so painful that you have to change." I have lived out this statement in my own life! Change is difficult. We want everything to stay the same. Old wine is much easier to drink, as Jesus said (Lk. 5:39). But God is in the business of change. If everything always stays the same we would never grow and mature. Change brings stress, however, and stress is not always fun to live with.

I have experienced intimately what stress is like to live with. I went through a serious burnout in the spring of 2001.

I love the church. I have given up my life on behalf of the church. I realize that God will treat us how we have treated the church. However, I don't like it when the church makes it hard for people to receive forgiveness and measure up to some religious set of standards. When we are more concerned about how people look than what their hearts are really like, we become like the Pharisees in the New Testament. We judge by outward standards yet God sees our hearts.

We have a few basic needs as human beings: to know and be known. How can we meet these needs unless we are willing to be transparent and honest with each other? We have applauded visionary leaders, but have missed out on the importance of relationships. Don't get me wrong, vision is important, but without authentic relationships, church becomes a place of doing and not being.

I was a visionary kind of leader, and I ended up burnt out and empty. I forgot about the simple things of life. Church is about people and not just slick programs. Each person has worth in God's eyes. I allowed my priorities to get all mixed up and my family and I paid the price. I became addicted to adrenaline and I ran on empty for far too long and went down in a flaming crash.

I now realize the need for authentic relationships and want to invest my life in people and not things. What do I mean by that last statement? I think that we are to build people and not just fulfill a vision.

I hope that as you read this book you will experience the comfort of the Holy Spirit, laugh out loud, and find hope to go on with your life. If all you can do today is breathe, that's okay. Most of the lessons that I have learned have come from true-life situations. I will attempt to share some experiences and stories with you to illustrate these truths. We need to learn to trust that God does have a process in mind and that process is right and good and will bring you to maturity in Him!

1

GIFTS ARE GIVEN
BUT FRUIT IS GROWN

"But the fruit of the Spirit is love, joy, peace, patience, kindness, goodness, faithfulness, gentleness and self-control. Against such things there is no law." (Gal. 5:22)

"And now these three remain: faith, hope and love. But the greatest of these is love. Follow the way of love and eagerly desire spiritual gifts, especially the gift of prophecy." (1Cor. 13:13-14:1)

Why can't the gifts of the Holy Spirit and the fruit of the Holy Spirit be linked together in harmony? There has been lots controversy over which are more important. We have allowed these precious things of the Spirit to divide the Body of Christ. Some denominations have placed a great emphasis on the fruits of the Holy Spirit in the believer's life, while others have had a much-needed emphasis on the gifts of the Holy Spirit in the believer's life. In this chapter I am going to explore this topic by discussing a few different experiences that I have had along the way, experiences that illustrate this very important point: The gifts and fruit of the Holy Spirit can come together in the life of the believer when they are based in love.

Here are a few questions to consider when we think of this topic: why can't we have both gifts and fruit operating at the same time? Why do we have to emphasize one over the other? Truth is we need to have both the gifts *and* the fruit operating in our lives to experience the fullness of God. Another question: why have we allowed the precious things of God to bring division in our midst?

Jesus seemed to think that love was very important.

"Let me give you a new command: Love one another. In the same way I loved you, you love one another. This is how everyone will recognize that you are my disciples--when they see the love you have for each other" (John 13:34, 35).

The world will not think that we are different because we can come up with a slick presentation; they will take notice as we love each other. When the gifts of God work together with the fruit of the Spirit there is an incredible expression of the Kingdom of God. This is what Sue and I experienced in Toronto at the Airport Vineyard Church. There were several things that attracted me to this church. The way they loved was incredible. It was one of the first places that I found where the gifts and the fruit were put together in their statement of faith:

"We believe the Holy Spirit lives in us as believers and brings love, joy, peace, patience, kindness, goodness, faithfulness, humility, and self-control into our lives. He works in and through us with His charismatic gifts. (Gal. 5:22-23; 1Cor. 12:7-11)" [1]

In 1992, God called Sue and I along with our three children to move to Toronto, Ontario. I was asked to be on staff at the Toronto Airport Vineyard Church as their first official Youth Pastor. We decided together as a family that God was calling us to Toronto. There is a huge difference between having the faith to take a step out into what God is calling you to do and actually doing it. I have found that it's fairly easy to talk about God's ways, but it's another thing to actually put them into practice in our everyday lives. We have taken many of these "steps of faith" over the years and they never seem to get any easier. I remember Gary Best, the leader of the Canadian Vineyard Churches, talking about steps of faith at the Langley Vineyard years ago. Gary likened these steps of faith to standing on the edge of a diving board ready to take the leap into the water. The pool does not look like it has any water in it to cushion the landing. There is only one way to see if there is indeed enough water to make the dive a pleasant experience: you have you jump off the board trusting that God will fill the pool.

We took the plunge off the diving board and found out that God not only filled the pool, but that the water overflowed all over the place. We would not have missed this Toronto experience for anything. We were very privileged to be a part of a renewal movement that was one of the most incredible experiences of our lives. God literally brought the nations of the world to Toronto to experience a renewing touch of His loving presence. Countless people went away changed forever by the presence and power of God.

I am not writing about these things to initiate a debate about the validity of the "Toronto Blessing" as it dubbed by the media. They are the ones that came up with that name, not us. It was a *God* blessing, not a Toronto Blessing. God was the one who was touching people and setting them free. Here are a few conclusions that I have come to over the years about our time in Toronto:

1. I would not have missed being there for anything; it was life-changing and the good fruit in our lives lasts to this day.

2. In any given church meeting, there are things of the flesh and things of the Spirit happening at the same time. The critics wanted to write the entire renewal movement off as not being from God. There is flesh involved every time we get together because we live in the flesh. Now, some people have taken sides on

this issue. I think these positions stem from a lack of discernment at times. We need to be wise and see what God is doing rather on what satan is doing.

3. Just because something makes me uncomfortable does not mean that it's not of God. It appears that when angels would show up and talk with people in the Bible, that they almost always had to tell the people to "fear not."

4. I wish that someone had informed me about the "desert season" in the life of the Christian. In fact, if you have been in a renewal/revival, chances are the next season that you may experience could be the desert. I spent many years wandering in the desert (metaphorically speaking) since Toronto; this is where God takes us and "speaks tenderly to us." (Hos. 2:14,15)

5. Miracles don't mature you in your faith; they are a sign that God is present. I love experiencing miracles, they are very encouraging. But what happens when God seems to not be performing miracles? Are we still going to serve Him? As John Arnott used to say, "We did not marry God for his money!"

6. 'Meetings' never replace meeting with the Father one on one. We need to cultivate a secret history with God and live from a place of rest, not activity.

There were many things that attracted us to the Airport Vineyard. John and Carol Arnott were amazing people, they loved us and we found incredible healing through being involved with them. I loved what the Vineyard Church stood for: "Walk in God's love and give it away." We were given the freedom to be who we were. We did not have to put on a fake spiritual front; we could be real and honest with where we were at in our lives. John used to say that **"God loves you just the way you are, but He loves you too much to let you stay the way you are."** There are things that John taught me that I still use today.

There were a few things that John valued as the Senior Pastor. He believed that leaders should be able to receive help as well as give help. Some leaders act as if everything is perfect in their lives, as is they have no needs.. We will pray for *you*, but *we* are fine. Here is a cute acrostic for the word fine: "Freaked out, Insecure, Neurotic, and Emotional." We are not always fine and have the same needs that everybody else has. Leaders used to be taught to keep their distance from their "parishioners." If the average church attendee knew that the leaders were just like them, they would loose confidence in the leader. This breeds distance and an unreality between the leader and the people.

John also believed that leaders needed to "walk with a little bit of a limp in the Kingdom of God." He was a little suspect of leaders who appeared perfect and had no problems. That limp or weakness showed that they were real and had lived life somewhat. The limp that leaders have is proof that God has been working in their lives. A limp is not a moral weakness; rather, it's an acknowledgement that without God in our lives we won't make it. (Gen. 32:31, 32)

John valued character first and giftedness second. God gives gifts to every single person in the entire world. These gifts are given freely and are not based on whether we deserve them or not. His gifts are based on His love for us. Romans 11:29, in the KJV translation, says: **"For the gifts and calling of God are without repentance.'** These gifts don't depend on whether we believe that God is real or not. He just gives them out. However, the working of the gift is meant to take place in relationship with God. Spiritual gifts are a wonderful addition to the life of the believer, but they do not keep you when the going gets tough. When crisis hits, your gifting may actually disappear, but your character will become evident through the crisis. That is why it's so important to be primarily focused on character issues. A lack of doing this is devastating the church. I am not saying that gifts are not important; they just need to be put in their correct place. I like this quote from Alan Medinger about character:

What is character?

"Character is a trait we don't hear discussed much

these days. Who talks of developing character in their sons; much less Christian character? What is character? It is that trait that reveals an internal and external consistency with a set of values.

A man of character holds to certain beliefs and his words and actions are consistent with those beliefs. He has integrity – a word that has the same root as integer – meaning one. He is singular in his approach to life. His internal life is consistent with what he appears to be. His words flow from honest convictions. His actions are determined, not by what is expedient, but by what is right.

To be this kind of man is to be strong, lacking in fear, disciplined, and if the values on which the character is built are sound, strength and discipline operate with gentleness and love. I heard a call to this kind of character in Paul's words to the Corinthians, "Be watchful, stand firm in your faith, be courageous, be strong. Let all that you do be done in love."[2]

I have heard another thought about character. Character is whom you are when you are all alone and the bright lights of public acclaim have been turned off. This is one of those statements that make you go *hmmm*. Public acclaim can be very seductive; it seems that everybody loves when you do what they want. Public opinion can change in a hurry, but

God's love and forgiveness last for eternity.

How is "fruit" grown in the life of the believer?

"Not only so, but we also rejoice in our sufferings, because we know that suffering produces perseverance; perseverance, character; and character, hope. And hope does not disappoint us, because God has poured out his love into our hearts by the Holy Spirit, whom he has given us" (Rom. 5:3-5).

"Consider it pure joy, my brothers, whenever you face trials of many kinds, because you know that the testing of your faith develops perseverance. Perseverance must finish its work so that you may be mature and complete, not lacking anything" (Jam. 1:2-4).

"Endure hardship as discipline; God is treating you as sons. For what son is not disciplined by his father? If you are not disciplined (and everyone undergoes discipline), then you are illegitimate children and not true sons. Moreover, we have all had human fathers who disciplined us and we respected them for it. How much more should we submit to the Father of our spirits and live! Our fathers disciplined us for a little while as they thought best; but God disciplines us for our good, that we may share in his

holiness. No discipline seems pleasant at the time, but painful. Later on, however, it produces a harvest of righteousness and peace for those who have been trained by it" (Heb. 12:7-11).

When discussing the fruit of the Spirit, it's very important to see that one of God's primary tasks is to bring us to maturity in Christ. God will allow circumstances in our lives to test our hearts; this testing is to see how our character development is coming along. The fruit of the Spirit is grown in our lives over time. Character is not just given to us; we mature into it. It's not grown in the good times when everything seems to come easy to us; it's accomplished during the tough times when it doesn't feel good to do the right thing. Character is grown when we make good decisions based on truth – when we don't always take the easy way out of life.

It's kind of like having a fruit tree to care for. You don't get mature fruit from the tree the first season. There are many things involved in caring for a tree. To begin with, it needs to be planted correctly: care needs to be taken when the hole is dug; the roots need room to spread out. The tree needs fertilizer to mature and grow. Of course there is also a time to prune the tree each year. There are many similarities between the care and feeding of a fruit tree and the care and feeding of a saint. It takes time, effort and patience to grow a tree. There is no shortcut to getting a tree to produce. After all, patience is one of the fruits of the Spirit.

"Fruit trees need pruning for two primary purposes: to establish the basic structure, and to provide light channels throughout the tree so that all the fruit can mature well. A well-pruned tree is easier to maintain and to harvest, and adds esthetic value to the home garden as well, but the primary reason for pruning is to ensure good access to sunlight. Did you ever notice that the best fruit always seems to be in the top of the tree? It's true, because that's where the most light is available. Training a tree that is open to the light, and easy to care for and to harvest, is the main consideration to keep in mind when pruning, whatever system you are using."[3]

This reminds me of my own trees at our previous home. Sue and I were finally able to buy a house after many years of waiting. It's was a very precious little house that the Father picked out for us. We had been waiting for what seemed like an eternity to get back into the housing market. Apparently God had not forgotten about His promises to us, although I tried to take matters into my own hands many times. It's was a perfect house for us and we loved our little hobbit house!

The back yard was full of fruit trees. We were able to have fresh plums, grapes, pears, apples, and a few cherries. When we bought the place all the trees were in need of a little tender loving care. The trees may not agree that I was being tender with them but that's not their business. Pruning may not be pleasant at the time but if done correctly it can reap a great harvest.

There is a lot more to home ownership than I remembered. I realized that I needed to prune all of the trees and the grapevine; they were getting unruly and were out of control. The cherry trees were the ones that really caught my full attention. Before they received my tender care they were both about fifty feet high. Both trees were loaded with lovely fruit, but the best cherries were too high up to pick. I also noticed that although the cherries looked fabulous they had little wiggly worms in them – not the most appealing treat at the best of times!

As the Fall progressed, I knew that these trees needed pruning in the worst kind of way. I must confess at this point that I had never pruned cherry trees before. I have been a pioneer in many different ministries, however, so I was not afraid to try something new. I went to my trusty home computer and researched how to prune cherry trees on the Internet. I found many sites that had valuable information on the process of pruning. Let me tell you that it's one thing to read about it, but it's entirely different when you start cutting the branches yourself. I realized that if this job was to be done right I was going to need to get some help.

I had a great neighbor who seemed to know how to prune

trees. My neighbor worked for the city and had to prune many trees in his career. He used to be a faller for a logging company. Fallers cut trees down for a living, Bill still likes to cut down trees. I think that he likes the sound and smell of the chainsaw. He got a faraway look in his eyes when I asked him about pruning the trees. Maybe he was thinking of the glory days of cutting huge trees down. Thanks to Bill, the cherry trees were pruned.

This was not your ordinary pruning job. Normally you are only supposed to take off about twenty percent each year. We took off about forty to forty five percent of the wood from the trees. There were some very curious looks from some of the neighbors when they saw the trees. We had to perform a radical pruning because they had not been taken care of for a number of years. We took away about eight big truckloads of branches. I couldn't believe how much wood was on the ground when we had finished. Bill is very good at pruning and about the best neighbor that a guy could have.

I am glad to report to you that both trees came back to life and have produced more fruit. No matter, the job had to be done. Now, all this reminds me of the pruning process in our lives. God has to prune us in order for us to bear better quality fruit that will last through the years.

We want the good fruit, but we don't want to go through the process to get it. But there is no other way; we must allow

God to work in our lives, pruning us, to bear even more fruit. There are two primary reasons for pruning: to bear a better quality of fruit and to keep the tree healthy. God does not prune us to hurt us; He loves us and knows what is best for us. God has our best intentions at heart and knows exactly when and where to prune. Instead of fighting the process, why not trust His process and embrace what He is doing in our lives?

The Vine and the Branches

"I am the true vine, and my Father is the gardener. He cuts off every branch in me that bears no fruit, while every branch that does bear fruit he prunes so that it will be even more fruitful. You are already clean because of the word I have spoken to you. Remain in me, and I will remain in you. No branch can bear fruit by itself; it must remain in the vine. Neither can you bear fruit unless you remain in me. I am the vine; you are the branches. If a man remains in me and I in him, he will bear much fruit; apart from me you can do nothing. If anyone does not remain in me, he is like a branch that is thrown away and withers; such branches are picked up, thrown into the fire and burned. If you remain in me and my words remain in you, ask whatever you wish, and it will be given you. This is to my Father's glory, that

you bear much fruit, showing yourselves to be my disciples" (John 15:1-8).

I am very happy as I read this scripture; I do not need to prune my own tree. God is the Gardener and we are not. We do not need to figure out what needs pruning. That is God's job. Our job is to make ourselves available to God so that He can prune us and make us even more fruitful. There are a few things that makes pruning more difficult in the life of the Christian, and one of them is to fight God as he gets the garden shears out to do the pruning.

What about the kind of fertilizer that a tree needs to grow tall and strong? The written word of God (*logos*) and the living word of God (*rhema*) are two of the ingredients that God uses as fertilizer in our lives. We need to read the word of God (Bible) and hear the word of God (from Him). John 10:27 (KJV) says, "My sheep hear my voice." So, we need to take time to hear what God is saying to us. We are changed when we tune in to the God Who loves us and Who wants to spend time with us. One meeting with Him can change us for a lifetime!

Just as there are the four seasons that make up the life cycle of a tree each year, so there are seasons in the life of a Christian. We need to become aware that there is a natural rhythm to life, and that it's cyclical in nature. There are times when God seems so close that we feel like we could reach out and touch Him. Then there are other times of wandering in the desert when it feels like He has forsaken us and gone away. Just as a fruit tree has times of growing and times of dormancy, we have these times as well; it's all part of the package.

How do we bring the gifts and fruit together in one place?

This is one of the age-old questions that have been asked numerous times and in numerous ways. I don't believe that I have all the answers that will solve this dilemma, but I do want to look at a few principles to help bring the gifts and fruit of the Spirit together.

1. Statement of Faith: Your particular statement of faith is like a foundation that a building is built upon. It's important to take time to build the foundation correctly or else you'll have to go back and repair it later. What does your statement of faith say, and do you actually practice the statement that you have articulated? When I found that the Airport Vineyard had the gifts and fruit together in the same sentence in their statement of faith, I sat up and took notice. In practical everyday life they lived out their faith. It was not a perfect church, but they tried to live out what they believed.

I have always felt like a bit of an outcast, I could never really fit in with the conservative church or the charismatic church. I felt way more comfortable walking down the middle – hence the need to bring the gifts and fruit of the Spirit together in one sentence. I have spent much time with both groups and see the richness in each tradition, but we are incomplete without each other, we each only have one piece of the puzzle. As my friend Hugh Fraser pointed out to me, "what you are really saying is that you desire to be part of the authentic church!"

2. *Act upon your beliefs:* What good is a well put-together faith statement if you don't live it out when reality sets in? It has been said, "Actions speak louder than words." The words that you believe are of vital importance but meaningless if you don't act upon them. Or as the old saying goes "if you talk the talk you've got to walk the walk."

Satan has about the best-developed theology in the entire world, but he certainly doesn't act upon what he knows to be true (Jam 2:19). He knows that Jesus is Lord and that "every knee will bow and every tongue will confess that Jesus is Lord," but his mission is to destroy everything that is of God.

I have been thinking about the abortion issue lately. I would say that there are a lot of different opinions about this issue. The Bible has a lot to say about the sanctity of life and that God has fearfully and wonderfully created us (Psa.139:14); God does not make junk. I come down solidly on the side of pro-life without a question, but I have some serious concerns about how we have pro-lifers have acted upon our convictions. If we are going to take a stand for pro-life then I believe that we have to have open arms to those who are contemplating abortions. We can't say one thing and do another, which is why the world has so often branded the church as hypocrites. We have got to be open to caring for unwed moms and not just rail against the system being wrong.

3. Love is the final answer: No matter what we discuss about the gifts of the Spirit or the fruit of the Spirit, love is the final answer. Look at what Paul had to say in 1 Corinthians about love. It's the foundation upon which everything else is built.

> **"If I speak in the tongues of men and of angels, but have not love, I am only a resounding gong or a clanging cymbal. If I have the gift of prophecy and can fathom all mysteries and all knowledge, and if I have a faith that can move mountains, but have not love, I am nothing. If I give all I possess to the poor and surrender my body to the flames, but have not love, I gain nothing" (1Cor 13:1-3).**

When is the last time you heard a resounding gong or a clanging cymbal? These days, my ears start to hurt when I listen to loud music. All those years of not taking care of my hearing has taken a toll on my hearing. A clanging cymbal makes a very high-pitched sound that's very hard on the ears. I fear at times that there is lots of cymbal noise when I go to speak or lead worship. I am not the most loving person sometimes; I still have many things that need to change in my life. It's a good thing that God is not finished with me yet.

Endnotes

1   Toronto Airport Christian Fellowship Statement of Faith
2   Healing and Growth – Homosexuality and Christian Character. Alan P Medinger
3   Pruning Tree Fruit - The Basics. Gary Moulton & Jacky King, WSU Mount Vernon Research & Extension Unit

2

GOD IS FAITHFUL

"Because of the Lord's great love we are not consumed, for His compassions never fail. They are new every morning; great is your faithfulness" (Lam 3:22, 23).

There have been times when I have doubted God's love and faithfulness. I am learning, however, that God's response to me never depends upon my behavior. He is always faithful, even when I'm not. God's faithfulness takes my breath away; He always follows through on His promises. God means what He says and it's impossible for Him to lie. (See Heb. 6:18.)

At one point in my life, I was working at my family's lumber business and was looking forward to getting more involved in the management end of things. At that point I believe that I received a call from God to go into full time ministry work. I realized that I first needed to get some schooling, so attended one year at Okanagan Bible College in Kelowna, B.C., and two years at Columbia Bible College in Abbotsford, B.C. These years were some of the hardest of our lives but some of the best as well. Sue and I started to live the life of faith from that time forward.

God called us to become involved in leadership in the Body of Christ, but we had no idea of the ramifications of our decision to say "yes" to God. One thing we did know: we didn't want to get to the end of our lives and have missed anything that God had for us. We were not going to let fear stand in our way; if God opened a door before us then we were going to walk through it, regardless of the personal cost involved.

It is one thing to believe that God is calling you to live by faith, but it's another thing to actually live this life of faith out daily.

I'm not about to suggest that we have not been through gut-wrenching times when we thought that God had abandoned us. We have. We spent far too much time questioning God's love for us, but found in every situation that He met us with His presence and love.

What is Biblical faith?

Look at the definition of faith from the dictionary: "Confident belief in the truth, value, or trustworthiness of a person, idea, or thing."[1] Faith has little to do with our emotions or feelings. Trust is a synonym for faith and when we say we have faith in something, we put our trust in this fact, believing it to be true. We then need to act upon that truth to build our faith.

"Now faith is being sure of what we hope for and certain of what we do not see. This is what the ancients were commended for" (Heb. 11:1, 2).

I have pondered these two verses for a long time. We are to be sure of what we hope for. I place my hope in the living Lord Jesus Christ today. I am certain that He is good and that he means what He says in Scripture. As an old saying says, "God said it; I believe it, that settles it."

"And without faith it is impossible to please God, because anyone who comes to him must believe that he exists and that he rewards those who earnestly seek him" (Heb. 11:6).

"All these people were still living by faith when they died. They did not receive the things promised; they only saw them and welcomed them from a distance. And they admitted that they were aliens and strangers on earth. People who say such things show that they are looking for a country of their own. If they had been thinking of the country they had left, they would have had opportunity to return. Instead, they were longing for a better country—a heavenly one. Therefore God is not ashamed to be called their God, for he has prepared a city for them" (Heb. 11:13-16).

Hebrews 11 is known as the Faith Chapter. The writer lists some of the Old Testament heroes to show the kind of faith that they had. They believed God even though they had not received their promises before they died. People like Abraham and Moses believed the promises that God gave them and they were commended for their faith. These "ancients" did not fail in their faith, but their faith rested in "Jehovah Jirah ("The Lord will provide"), who raises the dead.

God very seldom removes us from the trials that we face, but instead teaches us how to walk through the circumstances of life with grace and dignity. I am not talking about abusive situations where someone is being hurt or wounded, but about everyday life. Trials come to pass, they are not forever, and God will make a way through the trial.

I think that we have done a huge disservice to people by telling them that everything will work out in their lives if they "just believe in Jesus." They will "be blessed beyond measure and never have to face troubles or challenges again." "Life just gets better and better everyday as you stroll along with Jesus at your side." These statements are simply not the truth, Jesus promised us that we would face troubles in our lives, but that He has "overcome the world" (Jn. 16:33).

"Therefore, since we are surrounded by such a great cloud of witnesses, let us throw off everything that hinders and the sin that so easily entangles, and let us run with perseverance the race marked out for us. Let us fix our eyes on Jesus, the author and perfecter

of our faith, who for the joy set before him endured the cross, scorning its shame, and sat down at the right hand of the throne of God. Consider him who endured such opposition from sinful men, so that you will not grow weary and lose heart" (Heb. 12:1-3).

We need to take to heart and put into practice what this verse in Hebrews says. We are to "fix our eyes on Jesus" as our leader. Jesus paid the ultimate price for his perfect faithfulness to His Father. We can take heart from His example, to be obedient to God. Being a Christian is the hardest thing that I have ever done. It takes guts to believe when all around us seems to be falling apart. It's so much easier for us to chuck it all and live for ourselves, but in the long run living for ourselves will bring loneliness and destruction.

Our faith must not rest on the premise that God must answer every prayer exactly how we want Him to. Rather, we must put our faith in our loving Heavenly Father who knows exactly how we feel and cares for us in every situation. We must learn to be anchored to the bedrock of Scripture and to rest in the promises of God. Sometimes, God seems to be distant and silent, as if He has abandoned us, but the Bible says that He will "never leave us nor forsake us" (Heb. 13:5). There are many times when we must walk through life without seeing miracles, yet still trust that God is taking care of us. Miracles are a sign that God is in our midst, His

Kingdom is a present reality. Miracles are lovely, but they do not bring about maturity in a person's life. Miracles are meant to point us to the Miracle Maker, but too often we get hung up on *having* to see God's miraculous power to validate our lives.

The essence of faith is to believe without seeing.

I have come to realize that God is the One who provides for me and my family, the One who pays my wages. I am not a self-made man; God made me in His image and is helping me to mature and to become who He made me to be.

God is our provider; this must be settled in our hearts if we are to have peace in our lives. God is our sustainer and provider no matter what. As Christians we must rest in the fact that God is the One who upholds and sustains us, we can't do it on our own.

Who really provides for you?

My family and I moved to Toronto, Ontario in 1992. I became the Youth Pastor at the Toronto Airport Vineyard Church. We had no idea about the kind of adventure that we were embarking upon. If we had been told about all the hardships that we would face then we would never have moved to Toronto. I'm so glad that I don't have perfect vision to see every trial that I'm going to face: I would give up and stay locked in my house.

To start with, the church didn't have the funds in place to be able to pay us a full salary, yet we believed in our hearts that God was calling us to move to Toronto and be involved with this church. We decided to send out support letters to friends and family to ask for help in this new endeavor. People stepped forward and helped us out in very practical and gracious ways. The support that we received was not enough to make ends meet, "but God" had different plans.

I remember one Sunday the offering was way short at the church and I asked John Arnott, my senior pastor, "What are going to do?" He replied, "Pray."

God uses faithful people who give of their resources to support the work of ministry all over the earth. I have learned that money doesn't grow on trees; if it did I'd be the first one to plant a money tree and harvest that crop regularly. Our supply comes from the heart of a loving God who never runs short of resources. He seems to see things differently than we do, He's perfectly confident in His ability to provide for His children. As one of my dear friends, Eric McCooeye, tells me, "God will take care of all of your needs and some of your wants." [2]

There were more costs involved in starting a new life half way across Canada than we could have anticipated. The costs were not only financial in nature but emotional as well. We moved from a little town in southern B.C. called Yarrow, to downtown Brampton, Ontario. The population of Brampton at that time was about two hundred thousand and we were overwhelmed by the pace of life. The cost of living was considerably higher in Brampton; we didn't know these things when we were considering this step of faith.

There is only one way to take a step of faith. As the Nike ad says, "Just do it." Our dear friend Betty Griener told us during a prayer time that God knew everything that we needed and that He was going to take care of us completely. This was a promise that we clung to countless times over the two years that we lived in Ontario.

There were emotional costs to my family that we could never have anticipated. Imagine being taken from family and friends to a strange province that was completely new to us. Even the stores that we shopped at were different. We felt very lonely and homesick. We needed to learn to trust God with our lives – not easy thing to do but the best way to live.

The move was particularly hard on my wife Sue: she went through a very tough time being separated from all her friends and family. She had loved living in Yarrow. It was a very sweet little town, and she felt safe there. We moved to downtown Brampton, in an area where there were lots of rooming houses and drug deals going on. Sue put on a brave face, but she was very intimidated and frightened by the people that she saw in our neighborhood. She grew up in a Christian home where she was nurtured and protected, and she was not used to living in this kind of area.

Sue went into a deep depression and quit eating. Some people eat for comfort and some people quit eating when they feel depressed. Sue was a part of the latter group; she lost thirty-five pounds. That was not a good diet to go on. I began to get concerned for her and decided that I needed to pray. It's kind of funny that we go to prayer as a last resort. This depression lasted for about four months. It was not a fun time, but Sue made it! She came out of the depression with a new appreciation for the love of God and the truths found in Scripture. Here is one that was near and dear to her heart during this time:

"Be strong and courageous. Do not be afraid or terrified because of them, for the LORD your God goes with you; he will never leave you nor forsake you" (Deut. 31:6).

There was one particular day that was a breaking point for me. We didn't bring a vehicle with us from B.C. when we made our move. Some very generous people gave us the use of their slightly used cars. (Thank you to Gerald and John) Sometimes, however, free cars have things go wrong with them and these cars tended to want to carry on the repair tradition. One day I was driving in Brampton on the 410 Hwy, minding my own business. The car started to act up, kind of sputter and run roughly. I'm not much of a mechanic, but I do know the basics, and something was not right with the engine. I decided that I needed to get the car off the highway and on to the off ramp. The engine quit working and no matter what I did, it wouldn't respond to any of my gentle encouragements to start.

There was nothing I could do to get the car to start, and there was no one in sight to help me. I had to push the car up a "slight" incline which was not an easy thing to do by myself. There I was straining to get my free car off the road and out of harm's way. I actually thought about putting it *in* harm's way, giving it a quick and merciful end. There were lots of big trucks that would hardly even notice if they ran over the car. I knew that there was no way I could push this car by myself. Then I witnessed a modern-day miracle; a Good Samaritan pulled over and helped me push the car. I was speechless; someone actually cared about what had happened to me.

We ended up pushing the car for two very long blocks; they seemed to stretch on forever. It was then that I broke down; tears began to flow freely. I felt like a little boy that was lost and couldn't find his way home. I phoned my Senior Pastor John Arnott and he came and picked me up and took me to a local auto supply store. He was a very practical man;

he bought me a set of jumper cables. They were a gift from heaven, because up till then all I could do was weep and all I wanted to do was get my stuff, my family, and move back to Yarrow.

Have you ever heard the term "But God"? Those are two very important words in Scripture. So many times when the people of God had their backs against the wall – for e.g., in Gen. 50:20 – God came through and delivered them. That was exactly what He did for us as well. The only thing that I really knew at that point was that God was good and He had not brought us to Toronto to hurt us. After I stopped crying, I decided to thank God for the situation that we were in, and that made a big difference in my attitude toward living there.

I really dislike Christian clichés; they make life seem so easy. Yet, we *do* need to have an "attitude of gratitude" in everything we do and say. Paul instructs us to **"Be joyful always; pray continually; give thanks in all circumstances, for this is God's will for you in Christ Jesus"** (1Thess. 5:16-18). The verse doesn't say that we are to be thankful "for" everything but that we are to give thanks "in" everything. A saying that stuck with me from John Arnott was, "There are ten things wrong and a thousand things right; it's your choice what you are going to concentrate on." As I put this principle into practice, I found that my perspective changed drastically towards life and that I started to thank God for the bad times as well as the good times.

God is completely faithful, even when I am completely faithless!

Have you ever felt lost? Do you know what it's like to feel trapped a long way from home and to give up hope that God cares about you? Those were some of the thoughts that were going through my head and heart during this next story. The setting of the story was during the Christmas season in Toronto in 1993.

We spent the first Christmas in Toronto crying our eyes out and missing home terribly. I remember the kids having an awesome time opening their presents, but all Sue and I could do was feel sorry for ourselves. We dared not look at each other or else we would have come unglued. The kids had no idea what was going on; they were swept up in the joys of the season. I don't think that children are supposed to know those kinds of things; some things are just too heavy for them to carry emotionally.

We had made some amazing friends in Toronto; among them were a couple named Steve and Cathy Dudgeon. I can't even begin to say thank you to this family for all of the support they have sent our way over the years! Steve stopped by on that day and brought us some cool presents. But more significant than the presents were the kind words and hugs that he gave us. We dried our eyes and were grateful for the visit. God had not forgotten about us after all!

Steve and Cathy have a son named Ian; we became very close friends and spent lots of time together. Ian and I had lots of the same interests; golf, baseball, and music were just a few of them. I had formed a youth led leadership team and Ian was part of this team.

After spending that first Christmas in Brampton, we really wanted to return home for the next one. There was no way that we could afford to do this by just trying to scrimp and save with the salary of a youth pastor. My dear friend Blayne Griener was out in Toronto speaking at one of our youth conferences and felt like the Lord had given him a promise to tell us about. He said that we were to put aside a little money to use for this trip home. He believed that God was going to send us home that next Christmas and we were to relax and trust God to do that. It's easy to *talk* about trusting God, but harder to actually trust Him and relax. I decided to take God at his word and see what would happen.

After a couple of months, there were still no finances coming for our trip home, and I was getting a little restless. I was beginning to think that God did not care if we went home or not. It's kind of strange how we come to conclusions about God's character at times like that. He promised that He would take care of it and all I had to do was trust Him.

We assume things about God that are not true. Given the information that we had, we were way too quick to jump to conclusions about what would happen.

December rolled around and, let me tell you, I was not a fun guy to live with. There was still no money for this elusive trip home at Christmas. Why would God dangle a carrot in front of us, only to yank it away when we were trying to trust Him to provide? I became angry and bitter at that point. I chose to make the worst of a good situation. I remember being out on a bike ride and yelling at God. Why in the world would He promise us something and not deliver on it? I resigned myself to the fact that we would not be going home, and I came up with that famous denial statement, "It's no big deal." In actual fact, it *was* a big deal to me, but I had to do something with the pain of a broken promise.

About three weeks before Christmas, we were having a youth leadership meeting. There were about ten or twelve leaders in attendance; it was going to be a great time to hang out and talk about what the Lord had been doing in our lives. I was "the leader" and knew how this meeting ought to run. I took charge, which is what leaders are meant to do, but God had other plans!

My youth leaders had funny expressions on their faces, the kind that made me wonder what they knew that I did not. I knew these guys had something to say but I had no inkling of what it was. I thought that perhaps I had offended them and they needed to confront me about my behavior. I have been wrong many times, but this situation "took the cake."

My dear young friends produced a flight itinerary from behind their back like a magician pulls a rabbit out of a hat. I was stunned as I realized what they had done for me. These precious youth had put together the financing necessary to send us all on the plane to B.C. for Christmas. Sometimes I wondered what my youth leaders thought about us – yet they had gone more than the "extra mile" to bless us. I was absolutely speechless and all I could do was cry. (I did a lot of crying in Toronto over those two years!) It was at that point that God's loving voice broke through and spoke deep in my heart.

"When you are completely faithless I am completely faithful. I am always faithful and I never change. I said that you were going to be going home at Christmas and I always carry through on my promises."

I had been exposed as faithless in front of all of these people, yet they still loved me for who I was. That was the kindness of God and His people in action. They never gave up on us and blessed us beyond comprehension, even when we didn't deserve it!

I wish that I could say that I have never doubted God and His love since that day, but then I'd be telling a lie. I struggle to rest in His presence and trust His promises. Yet God still comes through every day on His promises to me, even if I don't always follow through with my end of the bargain. It's simply in the nature of God to love and bless his children. The hymn, *Great is Thy Faithfulness*, has deep meaning to me. Let's spend some time meditating on these words:

Great is Thy Faithfulness

Great is Thy faithfulness, O God my Father;

There is no shadow of turning with Thee;

Thou changest not, Thy compassions, they fail not;

As Thou hast been, Thou forever will be.

Great is Thy faithfulness!

Great is Thy faithfulness!

Morning by morning new mercies I see.

All I have needed Thy hand hath provided;

Great is Thy faithfulness, Lord, unto me!

Summer and winter and springtime and harvest,

Sun, moon and stars in their courses above

Join with all nature in manifold witness

To Thy great faithfulness, mercy and love.

Pardon for sin and a peace that endureth

Thine own dear presence to cheer and to guide;

Strength for today and bright hope for tomorrow,

Blessings all mine, with ten thousand beside![3]

Endnotes

1   Dictionary.com
2   From the many sayings of Eric McCooeye
3   Great is Thy Faithfulness – Words by Thomas O. Chisholm, Music by William M. Runyan

3

PILLARS IN THE CHURCH

I had the privilege of planting Freshwind Christian Fellowship in Abbotsford, B.C. with my dear friend, Brad Jersak. We decided to put all the 'How to plant a church' books on the shelf, and to instead rely on Jesus to guide us. After all, Jesus is the real leader of the church, not us. If Jesus is the leader of the church then we need to learn to hear His voice and obey what He says to us. He took us through many adventures of faith as we struck out and planted the church. One of those adventures was how He identified the pillars of Freshwind Church were.

One day Brad and I were at one of our favorite coffee shops, which doubled as our office. As we were sipping our drinks, a man with a proven prophetic gift came and sat with us. He looked me square in the eyes and told me that he had a prophetic word for our beloved little Freshwind Church, "the little Church that could." I trusted this person and was eager to hear what God had spoken to him.

He began by talking about the foundation of the church, saying that it was set and complete, but that God was now starting to erect the pillars. I was intrigued by the word-picture that he was painting; after all, the entire building rests on the foundation. The pillars are also important in that they hold the roof up. He then said that God had shown him in a vision that the four pillars were then set and the roof was placed on those pillars, but that there was flag of pride flying over the building. God was going to deal with this flag of pride in His own way and His own time. I had peace about this word and knew that God meant what He said: He would deal with it and I didn't need to lose sleep over it.

I began to contemplate what the four pillars of the church were; I assumed the pillars must be four of the male leaders in the church. Brad then suggested that perhaps our wives might be involved in making up these pillars as well. Of course he was right, our wives were an integral part of what God was doing.

I thought that we had reached the right conclusion for sure: the four men along with their wives made up the four pillars of the church. About a month went by and we were privileged to have a man named Bob Brasset visit us on a Sunday morning. He was sharing with us about the physical healing ministry, how God wants to heal today and how much He loves us. Physical healing is about His love and grace, not just about seeing some sort of miracle.

Pillar 1 – The Disabled

As Bob was speaking, he looked towards the people with disabilities in our church. He noticed one particular girl sitting in her wheelchair and asked what her name was. Unbeknownst to Bob, he had pointed to my older sister, Kathy. He had our attention; at that point all eyes were on him. We told him that her name was Kathy West and that she was my sister. Without any big fanfare Bob then replied that Kathy West was a pillar at Freshwind Church. I felt like I had been punched in the gut. I was shocked into silence, and felt like a little kid who had given the wrong answer in class.

Have you ever had one of those moments when you're completely exposed and you know that there is nothing to do except confess that you were totally wrong? God was speaking to my heart about His Kingdom and how it worked. If my sister Kathy was a pillar in the church then what exactly did these pillars mean to God? What were the other pillars in the church? As we waited, the Lord made it clear what the other pillars were.

Imagine that God had ordained my sister Kathy and all the other people with disabilities to be the first pillar in Freshwind. What does that say about the things that God values? I distinctly remember telling God that there was no way that we could build a church with these kinds of people. He must have had a good chuckle when he heard me say that. People with disabilities don't tithe so how can they be of use in the church? I found out that to be "of use" in the church is an irrelevant issue; it is God's church and He is the leader.

People have intrinsic value because God has created them, not because they can perform tasks. He doesn't need us for anything. He has no needs. However, He does want us to be involved in what He is doing. He invites us into a partnership with Him to reach out to the ones who need Him.

Imagine the first pillar: it consisted of people that could not hold anything up in the natural. They had little or no strength to perform the kinds of tasks that one would think that pillars normally perform. Perhaps people with disabilities are a symbol of something that God highly esteems in His Kingdom: those who are broken in spirit and contrite in heart. (See Psa. 34:18.)

When I think of my sister Kathy, the words *humility* and *transparency* come to mind. Kathy needs twenty-four hour care; she can't do many things for herself. But God takes care of the helpless, He cares for the "poor in spirit." The very Kingdom of God belongs to them (Mat. 5:3). Clearly then, these are some of the character traits that God highly values.

People with disabilities remind me of what Jesus taught about the great banquet in Luke 14:15-24. The Master wanted to put on a great banquet for his friends, but they all had other plans. They were too busy to come to the banquet. The Master was not impressed by their response so he told his servants to go out and invite the lame, the crippled, the blind and the lost—basically anyone who wanted to come. He wanted his table full for the great banquet. God highly values brokenness and humility, something that people with disabilities characterize in their everyday lives.

We learned over time to hear their responses as we met for church. People with disabilities speak a language; it may be English and it may not be. Nevertheless, they are speaking and we need to give them an equal place. They are members of the body of Christ and have the same standing that any other person has. Remember that although their bodies may be disabled, their spirits are not.

Pillar 2 - The Children

God highly values children; they are another group of marginalized people. (See Mat. 19:13-15.) Children are not only our future but our present as well. They have an important role in the church today. We need to include them in the life of the church today and not just in the future when they grow up.

There are a few character traits that come to me when I think of children. They are trusting. They haven't had years to build up bitterness. Children tend to have innocent spirits;

as they get older they lose this sense of innocence towards the world. Life crowds in on children, they start to face issues that they are not meant to face. By the time a child is a young teen, he or she can be incredibly cynical and wary of life; this comes from being assaulted by the media, peer pressure, or by broken family situations, to name just a few things.

The Bible tells us that we are to become like little children, innocent in the ways of the world and wise in the ways of God (See Mat. 18:1-5; Rom. 16:19.). We tend to be the exact opposite; we value worldly wisdom above knowing and loving God. The Bible instructs us to become child-like, but what does that mean?

I asked some of my friends what being childlike meant to them. They said that children are honest and are not bound by fear. Children live simple, fun lives. When you tell them something they believe it at face value. Why would someone lie to a child? Young children don't have the capacity for abstract thought. They think in concrete ways. You tell children that God is good and wants to be their friend and they will want to be friends with God most likely. If a child is told that God heals today, and someone is sick, he will pray for healing with full expectation because he was told the truth.

Children tend to have an innocent spirit about them. I'm not saying that they have no sin and don't need Jesus, but they just have this way about them that is not based in bitterness and cynicism. Something happens to children as they grow up: they begin to see that the world can be a nasty place where you can't trust everyone and there are mean people who do terrible things. By the time children reach early adolescence they can become incredibly wounded and damaged. It's a very sad commentary about our society.

Jesus taught his disciples that they were to become childlike, not childish. As I look around at the church it seems to me that we are more childish than childlike. We fight and argue to get our way, rather than preferring others over ourselves.

If God places such a high value on children, then we ought to as well; that was the bottom line for us. We value the fact that God speaks to his children and they listen to what He says. We need to give them a voice in the church, rather than shush them and get them out of the way because they are noisy.

Pillar 3 - The Prodigals

It seemed to us that God was saying that the prodigals were the third pillar at the church. There are a few different understandings of what this term means; to us it meant the over-churched, people who had grown up within the religious establishment and left for whatever reason.

Prodigals leave the church for so many different reasons. I think that God will allow people to go through these prodigal seasons to teach and train them. There's nothing like a good dose of reality to teach someone how good they actually had it.

Brad and I wanted to create an environment that welcomed 'whosoever' wanted to come and hang out. You didn't have to "sign on the dotted line" in order to belong; you just came out and were part of the community. We had lots of people who "strayed away from home" but somehow found their way back to the Father's house when they were ready. They didn't have to believe the "right things" in order to be accepted. These people were accepted for who they were and not what they believed. They needed love and care, not preaching that condemned them.

I have learned many lessons over the years and these lessons have become invaluable in everyday living. Here was an invaluable lesson that God taught me about prodigals: ***"Don't chase prodigals; when they're ready they will come home."*** I wish that I would have learned this lesson early in my Christian life; perhaps it would have saved me from many sleepless nights.

I thought that I was the person who would rescue these hurting people from their lives of despair, even though most of them did not even want rescuing. I used to say to young people that even if everyone else gave up on them I wouldn't; I would be there through thick and thin. This sounds very noble, doesn't it? Believe me when I say that all I did was get in the way of what God was trying to do. I ended up burned out and bitter that there was so little fruit in my ministry. I ended up resenting the very people that I was trying to help.

If you read the story of the prodigal son in Luke 15 it soon becomes apparent that the father gave the son his inheritance and let him go. You can't stop someone like this; you just have to turn them loose, hoping that one day they'll come back. It seems like they do return but they come back very different than when they left. There is level of brokenness that comes from living life that you can't teach—it just has to be experienced on a personal basis.

There were lots of prodigals at Freshwind CF and we realized that God wanted us to provide a place for them to come and be healed. They didn't have to do anything; there were no expectations on them. We wanted to love them and show them authentic Christianity. Most of them left the institutional church because they got tired and disillusioned by the business of church. Jesus didn't make all those sacrifices so that we could bicker over what color the choir robes should be or if we should let "those" kind of people be a part of our church. God is calling the prodigals back home and He wants the Body of Christ to open up the doors to let them in.

Pillar 4 – The Poor

"What finally counts is not whether we know Jesus and his words but whether we live our lives in the Spirit of Jesus. The Spirit of Jesus is the Spirit of Love. Jesus himself makes this clear when he speaks about the last judgment. There people will ask: "Lord, when did we see you hungry and feed you, or thirsty and give you drink?" and Jesus will answer: "In so far as you did this to one of the least ... of mine, you did it to me" (Matthew 25:37, 40).This is our great challenge and consolation. Jesus comes to us in the poor, the sick, the dying, the prisoners, the lonely, the disabled, the rejected. There we meet him, and there the door to God's house is opened for us."[1]

It is evident from Scripture that God loves the poor. We are not to judge people by their outward appearance or how much money that they make, but love people simply for whom they are. We are not to treat the rich better than the poor (Jam.2:1-4), yet this happens sometimes in church circles. I've heard many people say that "money talks." Yes, but my question is what does it have to say?

Does money show compassion to people who are hurting and who feel lost? I saw a bumper sticker the other day that read: "Whoever has the most toys when they die, wins!"

I'm not going to go on a rant against rich people or somehow elevate the status of the have nots above those who have, but like Paul, I would advise those who trust in their wealth to take stock of what is important in life (1 Tim. 6:17-19). Money may be able to provide a few creature comforts, but it can't buy joy.

The Bible says, "The joy of the Lord is your strength" (Neh. 8:10). We cannot receive strength from any amount of money. I have asked the Lord to test me with riches for many years, but I guess that He has decided that I wouldn't do well with lots of cash. Look at what the following verses say:

"Is not this the kind of fasting I have chosen: to loose the chains of injustice and untie the cords of the yoke, to set the oppressed free and break every yoke? Is it not to share your food with the hungry and to provide the poor wanderer with shelter—when you see the naked, to clothe him, and not to turn away from your own flesh and blood?" (Isa. 58:6-7)

"There will always be poor people in the land. Therefore I command you to be openhanded toward your brothers and toward the poor and needy in your land." (Deut. 15:11)

Favoritism Forbidden

"My brothers, as believers in our glorious Lord Jesus Christ, don't show favoritism. Suppose a man

comes into your meeting wearing a gold ring and fine clothes, and a poor man in shabby clothes also comes in. If you show special attention to the man wearing fine clothes and say, 'Here's a good seat for you,' but say to the poor man, 'You stand there' or 'Sit on the floor by my feet,' have you not discriminated among yourselves and become judges with evil thoughts?

Listen, my dear brothers: Has not God chosen those who are poor in the eyes of the world to be rich in faith and to inherit the kingdom he promised those who love him? But you have insulted the poor. Is it not the rich who are exploiting you? Are they not the ones who are dragging you into court? Are they not the ones who are slandering the noble name of him to whom you belong?

If you really keep the royal law found in Scripture, 'Love your neighbor as yourself,' you are doing right. But if you show favoritism, you sin and are convicted by the law as lawbreakers." (Jam. 2:1-9)

Jesus said, "The poor you will always have with you" (Mat. 26:11). They are a vital part of the Kingdom and we need to care for them. There are families in our midst that have needs that we could be involved in meeting, so let's reach out to them. This is by no means an exhaustive study of the poor or what the Bible has to say about them, I just wanted to share a little of how God led us to this last of the four pillars.

These are the firmly-established "pillars" at Freshwind Christian Fellowship. We did not choose them, but God made the choice very clear: "Embrace these pillars and I will embrace you." I am not saying that these are the only pillars that a church can have. However this is the way He led us at Freshwind. The main point was that He had these people groups in mind so they must carry some importance in His eyes.

Endnotes

1 Taken from Daily Devotional Emails: http://www.henrinouwen.org/

4

PEOPLE WITH DISABILITIES: REAL LIFE HEROES

"The LORD is close to the brokenhearted and saves those who are crushed in spirit" (Psa. 34:18).

Jesus is close to people with disabilities. They often live with a broken heart and most of them have experienced rejection and crushing their whole lives. His heart goes to the ones who are brokenhearted, the people who cannot help themselves. All people have worth to God, He created them and He loves them. How then do we respond to His invitation to love those with disabilities? This topic is very close to home for me, because I have a sister who has been extremely disabled from birth. I am going to spend some time writing honestly about what God has done in my heart towards people with disabilities.

Meet my older sister Kathy: she's a great girl. Kathy has spent all of her life in a wheelchair or lying horizontal in a bed. She was born with a number of birth defects—Spina Bifida and Hydrocephalus. Spina Bifida is apparently one of the most common of birth defects. It occurs during the first month of pregnancy and wreaks havoc in the development of the fetus. Hydrocephalus comes along with Spina Bifida and causes a blockage in the brain. The person's head begins to swell and a shunt must be put in to relieve pressure from the fluid build-up.

Kathy is just about the most fun-loving person there is and she is quite cheeky besides. If you were to meet Kathy you may think that she is just another one of those unfortunate souls with nothing to live for. This judgement could not be further from the truth. She is very gracious and kind and I would rather hang out with 'Chatty Kathy" than most other people I know.

When Kathy was born, my parents were told that she would live for only four to five years. I guess that God had other plans for Kathy. I was very excited to go to her fiftieth birth-day a couple of years ago. She has an incredibly strong and resilient spirit. She may struggle with physical and mental disabilities, but her spirit is not disabled at all. In fact, I think that I am more disabled than she is at times.

My Mom and Dad were told to give her up to the authorities when she was a little girl. They were told to treat Kathy as if she were not their own daughter; the government would take care of her. I am very thankful that the government has changed their policy towards disabled people. They came to the conclusion that these people have worth and that it would be better to de-institutionalize them. They brought people out of places like Woodlands and put them in homes where there is a sense of family. Kathy now receives individual care, and this has made a huge difference in my sister's life.

Can you imagine what happens to a person like Kathy when she has lived like this all her life? Kathy struggles. She doesn't understand why she can't see her family at times, but I have never known her to be bitter or to hold a grudge. Once in a while she will ask about things, but she never seems to dwell on the negative for very long. She deals with a lot of hard things every day that would seriously challenge my sanity.

Kathy was initially given to the authorities and grew up in a place called Woodlands. It was located in New Westminster, B.C., right next to the B.C. Penitentiary. Imagine a place where hundreds of disabled people were sent to because society didn't know what else to do with them. The old philosophy was to set up "institutions" to care for these people. Woodlands was a very impersonal institution, with several people to a room. The rooms were quite small so it made for cramped quarters.

Woodlands was a very scary place for a young boy. I knew that Kathy was my sister and that it was right to see her, but I never wanted to go there. I never knew what to say or how to act around her. Kathy's birth defects left her with some very noticeable physical and mental disabilities. She was among the first to receive a shunt in her brain; this shunt was used to drain the fluid that built up from around her brain. Kathy was very hard to understand and as a child I was afraid of the way that she looked. She had a very large head from the hydrocephalus and that really made me uncomfortable.

If Kathy was "retarded" then what did that make me? Since we were part of the same family did I look anything like her? How come she was "picked" to be born like this and not me? I had so many questions and lots of pain about my sister. My family was not good at sharing things that were close to their hearts, so I didn't get many answers to my questions. We would never talk about Kathy which was very hard to understand.

I went and saw Kathy until I was about twelve years old; after that I couldn't take going to Woodlands. I had no way to deal with the pain that I felt when I went there, so why even go? There was also no way to deal with all the anger I felt when I would go to Woodlands. I wonder how Kathy felt when we stopped going to see her? I know that she had the capacity understand that I was her brother and that I was not coming to see her anymore. It may have been complex for me to deal with but the issues were simple for her: "Why won't they come and see me?" Since I had no understanding of how to process my pain, I just stuffed it way down deep where I wouldn't feel it. This didn't work very well at all.

During my teen years I turned to drugs and alcohol to numb my pain, not a very wise choice.

Approximately twenty years went by and I had almost completely forgotten about Kathy. I was employed at that time as a Program Director at Columbia Bible Camp. The Camp is located in Columbia Valley up behind Cultus Lake, B.C. It was an incredible time for my family; I loved camp work except for the extremely long hours in the summer.

I was responsible for all of the programs that the camp ran during the year. I didn't have great organizational skills when I took the job, but I soon learned that to survive I was going to need to learn and grow in the administrative role! I was responsible for the annual Family Camp that was scheduled during the summer. The camp was six days long and had lots of awesome activities planned for the families that participated.

One of the activities that had been planned was to take people hiking up Mt. Cheam, which can be reached from the Chilliwack River Road. The hike is about two hours long and is a fair challenge for the average person. I was making my way up the mountain and I was having an awesome time surrounded by the most incredible view. I will never forget what happened next: God got my attention in a way that only He could do.

As you hike a mountain like Cheam, it's wise to take breaks

along the way. I sat down to take one of these breaks and the Lord seemed to tap me on the shoulder to get my attention. I have never heard the audible voice of God, but I am very open to His guidance and direction any way He wants to give it. I heard a voice way deep down in my heart ask me, "Don't you remember that you have a sister named Kathy?" I was undone, it felt like I had been hiding something from myself for all those years and with one question I was completely exposed. I sat and wept, overcome by the love behind the question, knowing that God had spoken to me. I knew that I had to get back in touch with Kathy and begin to get to know her as an adult.

How can I describe the range of emotions that went through my heart and mind? At first I tried to justify my behavior before God. How could I be held responsible for my sister's well-being? Was I my sister's keeper? Deep down I knew that I was caught and that God wanted me to contact her. It just so happened that my friend Ruth Langton started working with Kathy at one of the Mennonite Central Committee homes in Fort Langley. Isn't it incredible how God can put together circumstances that seem to just fit at the right time?

Ruth helped to initiate the first meeting that we had with Kathy. I hadn't seen her in about twenty years and didn't really know how to relate to her. I felt lots of anxiety going into that meeting, but I knew that God had instructed me to get together with her, so I went ahead with the meeting. Here is a scripture that God gave me about family:

"Is it not to share your food with the hungry and to provide the poor wanderer with shelter—when you see the naked, to clothe him, and not to turn away from your own flesh and blood?" (Isa. 58:7)

I came to realize that I had turned my back on my own flesh and blood, but I was willing to change and be in relationship again. I was a little apprehensive when I first saw Kathy because I couldn't understand her very well and had very little in common with her. None of those things mattered to Kathy. I was her little brother Brian and she loved me to pieces; that's all that really mattered to her.

Consider her life for a few moments with me. All she has known in life is either sitting in a wheel chair or lying down. From what I can gather, Kathy has never walked or ran one time in her life. The things that we take for granted in our everyday lives have escaped her. From the world's perspective she really has nothing to contribute to society. Kathy is an invalid. Since she can't do anything to add to society, she has no worth in the world's eyes. Perhaps that's too strong of a statement, but I know that there are lots of people who feel this way.

Have you ever thought about what the word **invalid** really means? A word like invalid is a label to put a person into a category; Kathy is not valid, she has no validity or meaning. I realize that the concise definition of invalid is "incapacitated by injury or illness," but the very nature of the word used to describe her devalues her person-hood. Words have the power to bless or to curse; these words are used without really thinking through what we are saying by using them. We devalue people like Kathy just by using these kinds of words. The old saying that "sticks and stones may break my bones, but names will never hurt me" is not a true statement at all. How many of us have been hurt by "mere words" that people have spoken to us?

I wonder what kind of value God the Father places on Kathy? Let's look at Psalm 139:13-18 and see what David had to say about the worth of individual people:

"For you created my inmost being; you knit me together in my mother's womb. I praise you because I am fearfully and wonderfully made; your works are wonderful, I know that full well. My frame was not hidden from you when I was made in the secret place. When I was woven together in the depths of the earth, your eyes saw my unformed body. All the days ordained for me were written in your book before one of them came to be. How precious to me are your thoughts, O God! How vast is the sum of them!

Were I to count them, they would outnumber the grains of sand. When I awake, I am still with you."

How good the love of God? I am glad that His promises are not based on my emotional, physical, or spiritual state. I am loved and accepted by God; He created me and breathed His life and love into me. Is my sister Kathy any different from any one of us, absolutely not! She is priceless to God because she is one of His children. God doesn't love her any more or any less than anyone else in the whole world. God fearfully and wonderfully made her and I need to treat her with the utmost respect.

I realize that by writing these thoughts out I am opening up more than one can of worms. I can hear some of the logical responses out there already: "That's nice that you feel that way about your sister, but if God is so loving how can He allow someone like Kathy to suffer in so many ways like she has? Why doesn't God come and heal her so that she can enjoy the rest of her life like a 'normal' person?" This reasoning leads to the ultimate question that people use to keep distance between them and God: "If God is so loving why does He allow suffering in our world today?" I would suggest that you pick up Philip Yancey's book called "*The Problem of Pain.*" He offers some very important insights into this topic.

Here is where I have come to when I think of Kathy: I love

her and am very proud of her. She's my big sister and I don't see her disabilities anymore; I just see a real cool person whom I can learn from. Here are some more thoughts for consideration. I have said them before, but they bear repeating: she may have some physical and mental difficulties but her spirit is not disabled! She is one of the most fun loving people that I know and I would way rather hang out with her than with some of the "beautiful" people in the world! I shudder to think of all that I would have missed out on if God had not gotten my attention on that mountain. Kathy has become one of my "real life heroes."

Kathy is very gifted in music; she can remember an incredible amount or lyrics from different songs. Music seems to be a gift that God has given to my family. My older brother Bob has been playing guitar for many years and is becoming an accomplished musician. I also play guitar and have been leading worship for over twenty five years. One of my favorite vocalists is Kathy. She loves to use her little egg shaker and sing her lungs out on my worship team. She lets me know at the end of the set that she worked really hard to sing even though she falls asleep and snores rather loudly at times.

Does she have perfect pitch when she sings? She's not even close to what we would call "in tune." I have an idea that what we value and what God values are two entirely different things. Does God have perfect pitch when He sings? What is true worship to God? It's a true expression of our hearts towards our heavenly Father. Kathy has become a true worship leader. People are inspired by her example of worshiping with all of her being.

There was one particular example of this worship-leading many years ago at Freshwind Christian Fellowship. We had invited Sherrine Cropley, a local soloist, to sing a couple of special songs for us. One of the songs that she chose to sing was "Amazing Grace." Sherrine has a very significant and rare gift to minister in music; she loves Jesus and sings from her heart every time I hear her. She sang this old hymn that day in only the way that she can. Kathy was sitting in her wheelchair and blurted out to no one particular that she knew that song! She started to sing along with Sherrine and there was not a dry eye in the place. Kathy became the message that God was trying to communicate with us.

Most choices have been taken away from Kathy. She needs total care twenty four-hours a day in order to survive. She needs someone to get her up, bathe her, change her diapers, feed her and most importantly, to make her coffee. Have I told you that one of her favorite things in life is a great big cup of coffee? She gets a major buzz from the caffeine and becomes a very funny girl. That's usually when the cheekiness sets in. Imagine all the choices and abilities we take for granted, that Kathy never gets to experience. In the face of such adversity she just keeps singing and smiling through life. When and if I grow up, I want to be just like my big sister.

A "Circle of Friends"

Kathy has an amazing network of friends who support her and love her. One of her favorite meetings during the week is called "Circle of Friends." It's a place where people with disabilities can meet with each other and with Jesus to have fun and be accepted for who they are. There is a time of worship, a short thought-provoking message, and then it's time for the refreshments. This particular circle of friends meets on Monday mornings at New Life Christian Reformed Church in Abbotsford BC.

On any given Monday there could be from 50-100 people in attendance. The circle includes people with disabilities, their care workers from various organizations and whoever else wants to be there. It is one of the most profound meetings that I have ever been to.

It doesn't matter what you look like, how much money you make, if you're short or tall, or if you can talk or not. There is no place for the world's standard of beauty here. People are treated with dignity and respect regardless of their station in life. It reminds me a little of the 1980's sitcom named "Cheers." One of the reasons for its popularity was the catchy theme song. "Cheers" was a neighborhood pub where people found real community. The analogy kind of ends there considering the basis of community was having a drink at a bar. The creators of the show found a topic that is near and dear to everyone – belonging.

This is what it's like to go to Circle of Friends. There is an acceptance of each other for the fact that we are human beings and not for being human doings. There is nothing that you can do to fix or change the way that the people with disabilities are; they just want to be loved and accepted for who they are. Just like Kathy, they all have worth as human beings because of God's love.

I have gone to Circle of Friends for a few years now and my heart is deeply touched almost every time I go. It's one of the few meetings that I will go out of my way to attend. As I drive up to the church I am overwhelmed with the sense of acceptance and love. As soon as I get to the front door there will be people there to greet me. I know that there will be people there who are genuinely glad to see me. I will get lots of hugs and handshakes from the residents. There are so many times that either laughter or tears come and sometimes both at the same time! It seems like people with disabilities don't generally have a hard time with hugs and physical touch. I won't be able to write about every person that attends, but here are a few of the countless "heroes" that come to mind:

Amanda makes me laugh out loud almost every time that I see her. She is such a precious person. She is one of the leaders and quite often will have a Scripture or prayer to offer. She has brought out many tears from the people present. Amanda knows Jesus and is not afraid to let everyone know that.

Then there is **Eddie**; he is a man of God. He knows Jesus and He wants other people to know Him as well. Eddie is one of the elders at Circle of Friends. You can tell by the way that he stands up front and directs people during the meeting that God has given him authority to lead. He seems to love to pray publicly for the food at snack time, thanking the Father for all of his amazing provision to us. (Our dear friend and elder Eddie passed away this last spring, we will miss him greatly!)

Linda is another person who comes to mind. Her birthday is one of the most important things in life to her. Linda knows that she was born in April, and the first question that she may ask you is if your birthday is in April. Her face lights up as she waits for your reply, anticipating the fact that you may be born in April as well. Linda is very exuberant at times and isn't afraid to show it. At one of the Circle of Friends meetings the worship leader asked if anyone knew the song,

Angels We have Heard on High. Linda exploded out of her chair and ran around the room exclaiming that she not only knew the song, but that she could sing it as well. I have never seen anyone so excited about life! She is a precious woman whom the Father adores!

Of course, I have to tell you about **Amber**, one of the cutest girls in the whole world. Amber had a bad fever when she was a little girl and there were very serious repercussions from it. Amber has to use a wheel chair to get around but that doesn't stop her much at all. She loves to jingle her keys; they make a happy sound, the kind of sound that makes her smile. Amber also loves to be close to those around her: she is incredibly affectionate. A day is brighter when you have received one of her hugs.

I could tell you about so many other people as well; they are all so fun to be with. These people truly are heroes in our midst. They haven't let their disabilities get in the way of their sweet spirits. They have not become bitter. God has put genuine simplicity into their spirits that touches me to the core. One question that you never hear from them is, "What do you do for a living?" They can sense if you love and accept them, they still have childlike innocence, and money or position doesn't mean very much to them.

It's important to realize that people with disabilities are no better or no worse than anybody else; they just are. It seems that society has wanted to push them away. We don't what to do with people who have disabilities. We don't know how to respond to them or how to treat them. They make us face the truth about ourselves, that none of us are immune from pain in our own lives, so why pretend that we are strong and have it all together? Imagine going through life with two and half strikes against you before you even get a chance to hit the ball.

There are so many things that can be learned from each other as we live together in community. These people know how to grieve; it isn't hard for them to be around people with pain, since they live with it everyday. They also know how to celebrate the simple things in life. Being with their friends is very important to them. God gives us opportunities to experience the deeper meaning of life by being in relationship with these precious ones.

Circle of Friends: A "Thin Place" between God and us

Circle of Friends is a "thin place" between God and us. The term "thin place" comes from the ancient Celts. "There is a Celtic saying that heaven and earth are only three feet apart, but in the thin places that distance is even smaller. A thin place is where the veil that separates heaven and earth is lifted and one is able to receive a glimpse of the glory of God. A contemporary poet, Sharlande Sledge, gives this description:

"Thin places," the Celts call this space,
Both seen and unseen,
Where the door between the world
And the next is cracked open for a moment
And the light is not all on the other side.
God shaped space. Holy.[1]

There is a special thing that happens when these people come together at Circle of Friends. Outward things seem to loose some of their meaning; they don't deserve our attention there. Who cares what someone else is wearing or what the latest fashion is? What *does* matter is that God the Father is near and that He loves His children. Who cares about what kind of a car I drive? How much money do I have in my savings account? All those questions are rather meaningless because they don't define who I am as a person.

Circle of Friends can be an overwhelming place for people that have not been around this kind of an environment. It can be very noisy at times, with all of our friends vocalizing in their own special language that God has given them. These vocalizations mean something; they are not just random sounds from invalids that can't communicate.

It took me a long time to become comfortable around this kind of setting. I have learned to listen with my heart and my ears to what is being said and not said.

I would encourage anyone to get involved with these

modern day heroes and see how much you will change along with our friends with disabilities.

Some Closing thoughts about these real life heroes:

- God created these people and we have so much to learn from them.

- They may have physical and mental disabilities but their spirits are not disabled.

- People with disabilities are very near to the heart of God and we need to treat them with kindness and respect.

- We need them in our lives more than they need us!

  "Brothers, think of what you were when you were called. Not many of you were wise by human standards; not many were influential; not many were of noble birth. But God chose the foolish things of the world to shame the wise; God chose the weak things of the world to shame the strong. He chose the lowly things of this world and the despised things—and the things that are not—to nullify the things that are, so that no one may boast before him." (1Cor. 26-29)

Endnotes

1   Sharlande Sledge, "Thin Places." Unpublished

5

BURN OUT OR RUST OUT

"In repentance and rest is your salvation, in quietness and trust is your strength, but you would have none of it" (Isa. 30:15).

I have heard a saying that goes something like this: "I would rather burn out than rust out." I bet the person that came up with that saying has never experienced a burnout. I went through my own private hell about five years ago and I never want to experience that again. I crashed and burned to such a degree that I started having mild panic attacks. Panic attacks are indicators that there is something wrong emotionally way deep down. I even started to forget words I was trying to say while holding conversations. I now see that I don't need to burnout or rust out (from inactivity), but learn to live and work from a place of peace and rest, not driven to perform.

The first panic attack happened while I was shopping at one of my favorite stores. This store has deals on experienced clothing and household goods that are second to none. I had taken my daughter Ashley out for a date; this was one of our favorite places to go. I was standing looking at some gem of a deal when my heart started to race and the walls started to close in on me, I felt a tremendous sense of panic rise inside of me. I knew that there was something wrong and that I better find out what was going on. I had never felt anything quite like it before.

I knew that if I didn't leave the store immediately I was going to have a serious meltdown. So I suggested to my daughter that it was time to leave—NOW! I didn't know what was happening, but I did know that I needed to get out of there and go home. I also realized that it was time to get some help. I decided that I had better run to God and ask for help rather than run away from Him. This time, working harder was not going to get me out of this situation. I was completely spent emotionally.

I phoned up a dear friend of mine who had gone through a similar experience and understood what I was going through. I needed help and I was not afraid to admit it. It was one of the best decisions that I have ever made. I met with him within a couple of days and he confirmed my suspicions. I was indeed burned out and ready to completely lose it. This meeting started me on an incredible journey that I am still on to this day. Before I describe this journey, let me explain what got me in this predicament in the beginning.

Graham Cooke says that the main reason that leaders burn

out is that they have not learned to live and minister from a place of rest. I can attest that this is a true statement from my own experience. I didn't know how to rest, but I was in for some very important lessons! *I was a man of God anointed with faith and power (or was that paste and flour?) for this final hour!*

Have you ever heard of the term *performance orientation*? This term describes the need that we have as human beings to perform well to be loved. We feel that if we perform just right then we will be loved and accepted. This performance mentality has absolutely taken over our society. Work hard, make your own way in the world and you will be esteemed and loved everywhere you go. After all doesn't it say in the Bible that "God helps those who help themselves?" I have been looking for that verse for a long time but I have never been able to find it. The reason I haven't found it is that it's not there! This is not God's heart for us. Look at what David wrote in the Psalms:

"The Lord is close to the brokenhearted and saves those who are crushed in spirit" (Psa. 34:18).

I'm not saying that hard work is wrong. I'm not saying that we should not put our best foot forward and give our best effort. I always want to try my best, but with performance orientation my best is simply not good enough. I have to try harder and do more things to make myself feel better. Good enough is never good enough. Imagine if performance orientation is mixed with deep emotional wounds: it creates a nasty breeding ground of deep pain in our lives.

This perfectly describes what I was like growing up. I am not pointing a finger of blame at any one person; it's just the way things are in our fallen world. I became a Christian on Thanksgiving Day in 1980. My life was radically changed from partying and doing drugs to serving the Lord. I felt a strong call to serve Jesus by helping people. I felt very drawn to young people and became involved in a church youth group. I loved hanging out with kids and being involved in their lives. After a number of years of volunteering, I felt a strong call from the Lord to prepare for full time ministry. Keep in mind, however, that there was always this gnawing pain deep in my heart to be loved and accepted for who I was and not just for what I did.

I was a terrible student in high school. I couldn't have cared less about the grades that I got. I was determined to "party hearty" till I dropped and "Who really gives a crap about life anyways?" I was trying to do something to deal with the pain that I felt. Addiction is one way of stopping the pain, it became a coping mechanism to help me get through the day. People usually deal with pain in one of two ways: they either stuff their pain down or they let it out in an unhealthy way. I think that I've tried a little of both at various times in my life.

I wanted people to come close but I couldn't let them in. As a result of all these things, I had a very distant relationship with my Dad. I stopped really sharing my heart with him from the time that I was about thirteen. Instead of taking my problems to my parents I retreated into a shell and hung out with my friends. They accepted me and loved me as long as I would party with them. I was an absolute wreck of person, but God had his hand on my life!

After becoming a Christian, I enrolled in Bible College in 1985 and began my preparation towards full time Christian work. Since my performance orientation was still alive and well, it affected me greatly in my studies. I did very well and it was a rich time of learning, but my heart's cry was still going unheard. ***Won't someone love me for who I am and not for what I can do?*** Of course, God loved me unconditionally but I didn't really take this truth into my heart. I had the right belief system but there was a huge gap between my head and my heart.

As I reflect on this thought about belief systems it occurs to me that Christianity is much more than just set beliefs. I went to Bible College to learn and grow in "the faith." I did learn and I did grow but I wonder sometimes if I came out with a head full of right theology and an empty heart towards the lost and hurting world? Of course, this is a question that is not easily answered. There's no trite theological response to explain the question away. I don't have any regrets about the time I spent at Bible College; I'm just asking questions to get at the truth.

Is it important to start with the correct premise about who God is? Absolutely!

Is it important to understand the basic tenants of the Christian faith? Without a doubt!

I believe that Christianity is as much a heart faith as it is a head faith. The "good news" of the gospel is that there is a loving heavenly Father who knows exactly what we are like and still loves us anyway! He's not ashamed of us and He doesn't have a big stick in His hand just waiting to thump us when we step out of line. As my friend John Arnott says, "God loves you just the way you are, but He loves you too much to let you stay the way you are."

As I became involved in helping real people with real problems, I witnessed this good news first hand. I saw God meet people where they were at and love them back to life—myself included. Can you imagine that leaders have the same needs as everybody else? This was a major revelation to me! **One of the main reasons that I burned out was that I tried to help everybody else and didn't take care of feeding my own spirit.** This is a very important issue in the life of a leader these days.

I spent many years working and ministering, too often in my own strength. That is the ability to pull your self up by the bootstraps and keep going no matter what. Through many different circumstances and just the natural progression of aging, my soul-strength started to wane. I began to notice a pattern of depletion over the years. I would be fine till about late May or early June and then I would start to "hit the wall" emotionally. I would be empty and need to take holidays and rest. But I couldn't realistically do that; after all, there were more people to save and set free. There were more places to go and preach the good news to the poor and the hurting. I was running on adrenaline and I didn't even know it. After all, God needed me to preach and to reach out to the poor and the lost, didn't He?

You can run on adrenaline for a long period of time but eventually it will all catch up to you and the outcome won't be pleasant!

Friends are like a tasty spice in our lives: they flavor us and make us sweat once in awhile. My friends are very spicy in-deed. My dear friend Brad came alongside me and informed me that I was going to take a sabbatical and I was going to take it *now*! I had two choices to make: I could keep work-ing and end up in the hospital, or I could take a sabbatical and get some much-needed rest. I trusted my friends and I ended up taking six months off. I had no idea how tired I was until I allowed myself to unwind. I remember a very spooky question that another friend of mine on Vancouver Island asked me. "If I allow myself to start to unwind, where will I end up?"

I faced this unwinding process and found out the answer to the question. I was unwound only as far as my loving Heavenly Father wanted to unwind me. I was completely at the mercy of God during this time, what a great place to be! Father God really is the kindest person I have ever met in my entire life. I have heard it said, "God will fix a fix to fix you. If you try and get out of the fix then He will fix another fix to fix you."

From my own experience I have found this to be a true statement. God finally had me where He wanted me, completely undone and ready to listen to His loving counsel from Isaiah 30:15. I desperately needed to rest and recuperate.

I started to go to my friend Trevor for counsel. I felt terrible waiting in the reception area of Trevor's office having to be the one that was asking for help. I was a leader and I was supposed to have the answer to everyone questions. It was so good for me to experience sitting on the other side of the desk. What an eye-opening experience! I had lost hope and was losing my mind in the process. Right from the start, Trevor was able to show me that the foundations in my life were in need of repair and needed to be fixed. I had believed lies that were operating in my life. I had allowed ministry to become more important than anything else.

Trevor asked me to prioritize my life. Where did my relationship with God come in this list? What about my family? Where did the church fit into the list? What I found out was that ministry had become my god. I talked about God being first, my family next and ministry following third. But in realty this was not true; I was living a lie. Ministry came first, God came sort of second or third and my family was not even a close third. I gave the best of my heart away to the people that I was ministering to. All my wife and children got were the crumbs that were left over at the end of the day.

It's very easy to live with lies; we all do it. We desperately need Jesus who is the truth to come and set us free. What I found out was that God wanted first place in my life again. He would not allow any idols to come in between us. I was captured by God's love again and I was completely undone. I was ready to face the truth and receive the help that I needed. This help came in the form of the "Pastor in Residence Program" that Trevor has been involved in at St. Matthew's Anglican Church.

The Pastor in Residence Program

How do I describe to you, the reader, the profound effect this program had in my life and the life of my family? I'll try and encapsulate in the next few pages what this program was and what happened in my life as a result of being involved with it.

The program was initially called "Priest in Residence" and was undertaken through the healing community of St. Matthew's Church. St. Mathew's is an Anglican church that embraces both the gifts and fruit of the Holy Spirit with one heart. The PIR is a hands-on approach to healing and restoring leaders that have, for one reason or another, been fried during the course of ministry.

Three other people have gone through this program and Trevor said it was one of the most profound ministries that the church has been involved in. Since I was not part of the Anglican Church it was decided that the program would be re-worked slightly and called "Pastor in Residence." We had a real sense that God was directing us to walk through this process together. I had no idea what I was getting myself into. This was to be one of the most intense and profound experiences of community that I have ever been involved in.

The PIR program works on a basis of real community. I thought that I had accountability before this time, but I was wrong. I had only experienced the kind of accountability where I could let people get close but only as close as I wanted them to be. Now I had lost control of my life and I was desperate enough to get the help that I needed. As a man it's quite hard to ask for help. "Help" is the kind of four-letter word that you will not hear most men say.

Trevor Walters, Rector at St.Matthews was my supervisor for the PIR. I am very much indebted to Trevor for walking with me from death back to life. I had a few initial tasks to complete as the program began. I had to come up with three or four names of friends that I could trust to participate in the group meetings. These meetings were held every three weeks. I didn't realize that I had asked four guys who were not about to let me get away with anything. I asked for help and they were more than willing to participate. Little did I know what I was getting myself into! My wife Sue was also invited to be a part of these meeting if she wanted to be.

The next task I had was to come up with three or four areas of my life that needed to change. This took some serious soul-searching. I had to become honest with myself and face up to some very painful things in my life. I came up with the following areas with lots of help from the people around me.

Objectives:

Give structure to the next six months. Begin to address patterns in my life that need to change. Take the first three months for reflection and healing and the next three months to work back into ministry opportunities. I am committed to the process of healing.

Goals:

Goal # 1 - I want to change my overdeveloped sense of responsibility (burden bearing).

I will not carry everything on my shoulders. I will not resent it when people won't help out. (That becomes a double bind. I have projected that people will fail me and thus they do.) I will learn what my gifting really is and what it means to live that out. I will learn to give the gift of my time to people, but not to everyone. It's my choice.

Goal #2 - I want life with Sue and my family to be fun and fulfilling again.

I will not use Sue as a personal dumping station for my anger. I will give Sue the space to be who she is. I will give the best of my heart to my family first. I am going to spend time with Sue. Go on walks and out for dates. I am going to continue to spend time with my kids. Take them out to movies and other activities.

Goal #3 - I want to learn the difference between being and doing (performance orientation).

I will not sell myself short anymore. I will learn to say "no" to invitations when I sense that my motivation is wrong (financial, a sense of being driven, fear, performance). I am not obligated to respond to every need I see by discerning everyone's heart. (I am not responsible to fix, solve and heal everybody). I will learn to carry the light end of things.

Goal #4 - I want to become resilient in my spirit.

I will be in ministry (life) for the long haul. It's a marathon and not a sprint. I will take proper holidays and time off each year. I used to think that ministry trips were like holidays, but they are not. I will have rest and recreation in my life (fly-fishing etc.) I am human and have needs.

After I came up with these objectives and goals, I had to negotiate with my "accountability group" to make the goals achievable and measurable. That was a very painful process because they wouldn't let me squirm out of anything. Imagine sitting in a room with all eyes on you, having to come up with honest answers to the questions that you're being asked. It was very unnerving. I had to be real; these guys could see right through me.

This process of negotiation took about three meetings. I had to boil the goals down until they were achievable. What good would goals be if they didn't bring about change in my life? This may sound like a benign intellectual exercise but believe me it was gut-wrenching. I was exposed for who I really was. My life was not going well and now they all knew it. However, I received nothing but love and care from these guys.

After having completed the objectives and goals, we started

to walk together through the process of the Pastor in Residence. I chose to hang out at Friends Langley Vineyard Church. It was so good to be able to attend there with no strings attached. I was not responsible to do anything for anyone for at least the first three months of my sabbatical. My friend Jessie made it very clear that I was not to be praying for or counseling anyone at that point. I was there to rest and get filled back up. This church was very healing for me and I am grateful for this community of faith.

As I have said previously, we had meetings with all the guys every three weeks. There were many times that I would be filled with dread as I was thinking of going. I was going to have to be real and not hide my sin. The first meeting was great; it was more of an introductory time. Trevor was the supervisor and he explained the parameters of the program. He would also watch over me during the meetings; if I'd had enough then he would end the meeting in his discreet kind of way. There was a sense from that meeting that this was the right thing to do and that we were in for some interesting times together. The second meeting was a little different.

The meeting started with me sharing my heart about how things were going during the last three weeks and how I was progressing with the goals. Sue was also invited to speak from her perspective about how things were going at home. Our wives know the real truth about us guys, we can't hide from them for very long. We may put on a real slick front in public, but they know us intimately. I shared my heart for about half an hour and then the questions began.

Jason observed something in my life and asked me about it. "Brian, how much are you worth?" If ever I have taken a question completely wrong it was this one. I thought he was asking how much money I make or what am I worth when I go on ministry trip. What he really meant was how much does God value me as his son? This question set me off for the rest of the meeting. I was very angry and let them know it. "What do you mean what am I worth?" *Not much* is what came to mind. I started to really steam and could have sworn my head right off of my neck. I had sacrificed and sold myself short for so long, I didn't know any other way to live.

I left that meeting with lots of anger. I got out of the car about half way home and yelled at God the rest of the way. It really helped me to get the stuff out of my heart in a safe place. The funny thing was that God didn't hold it against me; He just loved me with His unconditional love. He was allowing me to speak from my heart and not from my head. I was very tired of having to be so good all the time. He seemed to say that only one person was good and that was His Son Jesus. I was tired of having to always be the responsible one and make sure that everything ran well. There is a saying that goes something like this: God will overload your structures in order to heal you of life's hurts.

We have choices to make throughout our lives. We can choose to listen and respond to the kind messenger that God sends our way, or we can stubbornly go our own way. God will then have to get our attention through the hard messenger, and that can be a little scary at times. I have experienced both the kind and hard messenger over the years. I think that I am listening to the kind messenger more than the hard one these days. I made the choice to listen to my friends and change my life.

I would meet with Trevor the next day after these meetings. It would be a time to debrief from the meeting and evaluate how I was doing with my goals. There were lots of times when I was ready to throw in the towel and quit. It was just too hard to keep going. They were extremely stressful, and it took a number of months, but I finally started to welcome the scrutiny in my life. I knew that my guys had my best interests at heart, so I could trust them even when I didn't always understand where they were coming from.

As the months progressed we developed an amazing sense of community. It became apparent that I was not the only one that God was dealing with during these meetings. The other guys started to participate in the process of looking at their own wounds as well. That is what happens when we get involved with people: we get changed in the process as well.

The Pastor in Residence Program forced me to face many things about myself. I needed to take stock of my life and make some very important changes. I remember another meeting that was a changing point in my life. The day of these meetings with the guys could be very stressful. I never knew what I was going to face and that caused lots of anxiety.

Have you ever found that life is not very convenient? I was in the middle of a burnout and having to deal with teenagers at the same time. There were days when I felt like giving up. There were times when I could've quit everything, including my faith. I tried chucking my faith but it was like a boomerang, it just came right back. I realized that even this was about God's grace and mercy and not my faith. He sustained me through His love and patience.

I had a hard day with one of my kids. I was angry when I arrived at the meeting and I was in no mood to talk. I had no choice so I just yakked about nothing in particular for about three quarters of an hour. Everyone was intently listening to what I had to say. Keep in mind that all of these guys were straight shooters; they didn't hold back if they felt that I needed to hear what they had to say. One of the guys stopped me in mid-sentence and asked me what I was so mad about. He could tell that I was upset but I was trying to hide it from them. What was I thinking trying to hide from people who loved me?

I just let all the anger tumble out. I was so afraid to let them see the real me. I was sure that if they found out who I really was, these guys would turn their backs on me. I wouldn't be accepted for who I was; I had already made my mind up. I told them about the fight I had with one of my kids. I was feeling guilty and sad and felt like such a loser. I told them that I realized that my kids were going to have to go for counseling since I was such a lousy father. Their response shook me to the core.

They confronted me in love and asked what made me think that I had the corner on being a bad father? I was no worse than them or no better; we were all the same and all of our children might need help at one time or another during their lives. It was a major revelation to me that these guys **knew the worst about me and still really loved me.**

This is one of the lies that assaults us and keep us separated from each other. If people really knew what we were like with all of our "wrinkles" showing, they would hate us and not want us to be part of the community. That isn't the truth, but it's how we feel at times. Besides, it seems that everyone feels like this so why not expose the lie and get on with being real with each other? Being transparent can break down the walls that distance us. These walls keep us from loving each other and growing in grace towards each other. **I say, let those walls come down in Jesus name!**

That meeting was a turning point in the healing process on several levels. I didn't need to hide my "stuff" from my friends anymore. I was not the worst person in the world; there were others just like me. I wasn't condemned for my sin but forgiven and supported in the healing process. If this were all true then perhaps there was light at the end of tunnel! I could make it out of the black hole that I felt I was in sometimes.

Invariably the question would come up about how I was going to take care of myself and not burn out again. Here are a few of the safeguards that I have put in place that may be of some help to you:

- I will take regular days off and I am not available on those days unless it's something that is very very important.

- I will not live on the treadmill anymore; that's my choice to make. (Have you noticed you don't get very far when living on the treadmill, anyway?)

- I am only one person and I can't save the world! I can't even save myself! I can, however, help one person at a time; this attitude really takes the pressure off.

- God has given me (us all) a gift of time. I don't need to give of my time to anybody and everybody. I can give someone a gift of my time; it's my choice.

- I am called to mentor and equip, I am not called to fix! (Ephesians 4:11-13)

- I will not chase prodigals anymore. They need to come back of their own free will or else it doesn't seem to work for them in the long run anyway.

- I will surround myself with people who are honest and will tell me when I'm doing too much. I will listen to them and heed their advice.

- I do not need to accept every invitation that comes along. God will supply all of my needs and some of my wants so why not trust Him to do that?

Reflecting back on the way I felt afterwards, I can hardly believe I was even burned out. God has not only healed and set me free, but He has given me tools for living that I use every day. Do I still have bad days? You bet! Do I feel lousy sometimes? Yes, I do, but I know that when I feel like that I have been putting in too many hours. I am able to stop and take inventory of my life and I allow myself a regular Sabbath now. With God's grace I am not ever going to visit this painful place called burnout again!

6

CONFESSIONS OF A FREQUENT TALKER

"My dear brothers, take note of this: Everyone should be quick to listen, slow to speak and slow to become angry, for man's anger does not bring about the righteous life that God desires" (James 1:19).

I am guilty of doing the exact opposite of what James wrote in the above verse. I am slow to listen, quick to speak and even quicker to become angry. I have to deal with these weaknesses of my flesh everyday. There are times when I wonder how God puts up with me. Where can I go to find help with all this stuff? I find my help in the Lord; I go and ask Him to deal with me. Hopefully I am becoming a better listener, but I need to confess that I'm still not that good at it.

People have told me that I am a gifted communicator. I find that I would rather talk about my situation than have to listen to someone else. Listening takes discipline, and self-discipline is not always easy. However, I realize that at times my words have become weapons that have wounded people and I am sorry for what I have done, and see the need to change.

"We should all know this: that listening, not talking, is the gifted and great role, and the imaginative role. And the true listener is much more beloved, magnetic than the talker, and he is more effective and learns more and does more good."[1]

How do you feel about people who tell you what you should be doing instead of listening to you? Perhaps you're able to tune them out like you might a teacher in school, or a parent that keeps harping about something you may have done wrong. The problem is it's hard to tune them out all the time. Tellers like to tell you what to do and how to do it, but they don't always like to take their own advice.

A dictionary will tell you that a teller is someone who works in a bank with money, but a teller can also be a person who is often ready to give a word of advice no matter what the other person needs. They often "tell it like it is" from their particular perspective. Spending time with that kind of a person can become very tiring.

It's easy to mix up a prophetic/discernment gift with this type of telling. Sometimes prophetic people are tellers. Prophetic people may not be the best at listening, and may like to tell you what they are seeing, rather than just being quiet and listening. One of the first tasks of the prophetic gifting is to _pray/intercede for situations_ rather than speak about what they are receiving from God. Another important task of the prophetic person is to *teach other people how to hear the voice of God.* There is a time and place to tell the truth; it always needs to be mixed with kindness and compassion. (See Prov. 25:11; Eph. 4:15a.)

Look at how the Apostle Paul defines prophetic ministry from first Corinthians chapter fourteen. We are to build people up and not tear them down!

"Follow the way of love and eagerly desire spiritual gifts, especially the gift of prophecy. For anyone who speaks in a tongue does not speak to men but to God. Indeed, no one understands him; he utters mysteries with his spirit. But everyone who prophesies speaks to men for their *strengthening, encouragement and comfort*" (1Cor. 14:1-3).

I have had to face the truth about myself: I have been this kind of a *teller* most of my life. God has given me the ability to "see" into situations and perceive what is really going on. But I'm not very good at looking at situations through the grid of the incredible love of God. I more often look through my own judgement and pain – and this has caused many problems in relationships over the years. I often see what is wrong, rather than what is right in a person's life.

I came to this realization through a painful process during the "Pastor in Residence" program that I participated in (See the chapter on Leadership Burnout). During this time I was in a very vulnerable place. I was extremely fragile emotionally and

I would have panic attacks over the silliest things. If someone that I didn't trust got too close, I could be pushed over the edge. My heart would start pounding and I would be faced with irrational fear. It made no sense at all, yet it was very real.

I spent time with people that I would describe as tellers. It was very painful to be told "all the right answers" rather than just listening to me. I could not hear what these people were saying; I was in too much pain. I talked to my supervisor for the PIR program and he explained to me this kind of personality. I realized that I was angry and just needed someone to listen to me.

I can identify with Charlie Brown from the Peanuts cartoon Christmas special when he felt like everyone was ignoring him and what he wanted to say. For once Charlie just wanted someone to listen to him. I had listened to people for years and wanted someone to do the same for me.

I had a huge revelation during this time: I had needs and my needs were just as important as those of everyone else. I wanted to be able to talk with someone about the issues of my life. I believed that I had no one to talk with so I had to deal with it by myself. As a leader, I never realized that if my needs went unmet for a prolonged period of time, I would eventually have to deal with the fallout. Fortunately God cares for me deeply and provided people to care for me with no strings attached.

Painted into a corner

I came home from this meeting with Trevor feeling listened to and appreciated. I was grateful that someone was willing to walk alongside me, not judge me, just listen and point out a few truths in the process. When I got home, my sweet wife Sue was there to greet me at the door with love and kindness.

As I stood in the kitchen, I started to discern that Sue was carrying something in her heart. I thought that she needed me to tell her what she was struggling with. I proceeded to tell her how she was feeling. I painted her into a corner with my words: all she could do was agree with me. At that moment, Jesus broke through with a statement that cut me to the heart. He made it very clear to me that I had in fact been a teller most of the years of our marriage. I felt terrible; I had just done the exact thing that I had so recently resented in other people.

I was exposed for who I really was: I did the very thing that I despised other people for doing. I could tell other people what to do, but I did not follow through on what I said. It was an awful experience, but not half as bad as my wife had been feeling for most of the years of our marriage. It was time for me to admit that I was wrong – which I didn't want to do. Even as I write this, I can feel the grief of seeing and understanding what I had become. But God and my wife are very merciful and they both forgave me.

The good news is that God is so kind that he gave me the choice of responding in humility and repentance, which I did right away. There is nothing like learning a lesson in the school of hard knocks. Once you have learned it, you most likely won't forget and go back to your original behavior. Sue was very gracious to forgive me, which I was deeply grateful for.

Have I completely changed from being this kind of an insensitive teller? No I have not; I am still very much a work in process and always will be. I am growing and changing; things are always getting better, and there is always forgiveness at the cross of Jesus Christ. I can't change the past but I can change the present and the future! With God's grace and mercy I am becoming less of a teller and more of a listener.

Moving on to Maturity in Christ

If we continue to tell people what to do and how to do it, they will never have to mature and stand on their own two feet. It's time to stop spoon-feeding people and give opportunity for them to mature. Instead of telling people what to do all the time, we need to listen to them. We need to give people a chance to say what is on their hearts before we jump in the right thing to say. We also must teach them how to ask the right questions that lead to good, healthy behavior. People need to come to their own conclusions. Besides, it's not nice to "should" on people all the time. They need freedom to learn and grow at their own pace.

I'll never forget the first time that someone told me that I was doing this. I was out for a coffee appointment with someone and I "shoulded" on him. I told him what he should and shouldn't be doing. He felt trapped and told me not to should on him.

It became clear that I had once again painted another person into a corner with my words. There are better ways to go about telling someone something than *shoulding* on them.

Teaching people how to ask the right questions is a little like the principle that is found in this ancient Chinese proverb about fishing: "Give a man a fish and you have fed him for today. Teach a man to fish and you have fed him for a lifetime" (Author unknown). Teach a person to ask the right questions about the right topic and they will be able to grow and mature for the rest of their lives.

The questions we ask, however, need to be based upon the truth found in scripture and not on our fears. When we allow fear to control us, we're not agreeing with God and what is written in the Bible. "There is no fear in love. But perfect love drives out fear, because fear has to do with punishment. **The one who fears is not made perfect in love**" (1Jn. 4:18)

What would be an example of fear-based questions? They may look something   like this: What if I don't make the sports team that I have my heart set on? If I don't have enough money for retirement, what's going to happen? What if I trust God and He lets me down like everyone else has?

Wrong questions asked from wrong motives based on the wrong premise can become obsessive questions that take us to a very bad place emotionally. There is often no answer to these kinds of questions. "What if" questions can take us into very harmful thought loops; we spin round and round without finding any solid answers. These thought loops make us spin around in our heads and can leave us feeling confused and hopeless. How do we find answers to these fear-based questions?

Since they are based more on fear than truth, there is no good way to find answers. Almost one hundred percent of our fears will never come true. I find that a lot of Christians have a fear-based understanding of God and life. How can we continue to grow into the abundant life that Christ promised us if we keep embracing fear?

But the good news is that there are some "what if" questions that have the potential to take us to a good place in our hearts.

- What if God is really who He says He is?

- What if I never have to worry about another thing in

my life as long as I live because God has everything under control? (How then would I live my life?)

- What if God really does exist and He really does love me? What difference would that make?

- What would happen if I started to act on the things that I believe to be true? How would I live my life if I really believed Matthew 6:33? ("Seek first the kingdom of God and His righteousness and all these things will be added to you.")

What happens to you when you face a crisis? Do you run to God and trust Him to take care of you, or do you panic and run away from Him? Fight-or-flight mechanisms are turned on when we face difficult times. It would be easier to run away and not face up to the conflict or crisis rather than to stay and work through whatever is happening. These mechanisms are very obvious in the church at the present time. For whatever reason, it seems that it's easier to run away from problems and go to another church than face up to them and grow through them. I am not saying that this will work for every situation, but we run away far too often and miss out on opportunities for growth.

I believe that God really exists and is kind and loving to me everyday. I believe that God listens to me and cares about what I have to say. I believe that he will take care of all of my needs and some of my wants. I believe that He will never lie to me and follow through on all His promises that He has made in scripture to me. I believe that He always wants the best for me in my life and that He has a perfect understanding of what I need. I believe that God always hears my prayers and that He is always mindful of me everyday.

Since He knows me and what I need I can live at peace in my heart. I can learn to listen to Him rather than listening to my fears or wounding. He knows what is best for me and how I struggle, He cares for those that are "broken hearted and crushed in spirit." (Ps. 34:10)

If this is all true then I don't always need to be the one that is talking. As Paul Tillich said "The first duty of love is to listen."[2] According to Tillich listening to someone else is a truly loving thing to do. Not merely listening and formulating the answer we are going to give them when their lips stop moving, but listening with our hearts engaged.

"Listening is a magnetic and strange thing, a creative force... When we are listened to, it creates us, makes us unfold and expand. Ideas actually begin to grow within us and come to life... When we listen to people there is an alternating current, and this recharges us so that we never get tired of each other... and it is this little creative fountain inside us that begins to spring and cast up new thoughts and unexpected laughter and wisdom. ...Well, it is when people really listen to us, with quiet fascinated attention, that the little fountain begins to work again, to accelerate in the most surprising way."[3]

Listening then is at the heart of every relationship. You may be thinking that you don't have a gift for listening to people. I don't think that the ability to listen to someone is only about gifting. If you find it hard to listen, ask God to help you with it. Take sometime to consider what it feels like when someone listens to you and then do the same for someone else.

You might also be thinking that you won't know what to say after the person has had their say. That's okay, most people can work out their own problems after they have been able to voice there opinions or problems. Remember that God is still in control and will give you what you need when you need it. So why not take some time right now and listen to Him? (John 10:3-5).

Endnotes

1   Brenda Ueland *"Strength To Your Sword Arm: Selected Writings by Brenda Ueland." Copyright 1992* (American Feminist and Author 1891-1985)
2   *O Magazine, February 2004 US (German-born) Protestant theologian (1886 - 1965)*
3   *Ibid,* Brenda Ueland

7

LEARNING TO FACE FEARS

"Trust in the LORD with all your heart and lean not on your own understanding; in all your ways acknowledge him, and he will make your paths straight" (Prov. 3:5, 6)

Recently, God has been speaking to me about the fork in the road of life that we all face each day. We need to learn to make a good choice as to which road we are going to walk down. One road is called Faith and the other is called Fear, and it is up to us to choose which one we will journey down.

We can't stay where we are; we must choose one of the roads to journey down. Each road has it own set of challenges. When we choose to walk down the road called Fear we will face hardships without a sense of peace and assurance. Fear then has a chance to control our lives. Jesus still walks with us but we make the journey harder on ourselves. When we choose the road called Faith we walk it hand in hand with Jesus. Trusting Jesus is not a magic formula that will save us from hardships, but He will face these hardships together and bring us meaning in the midst of life.

There have been many days that I have started out walking on the faith road, only to let fear take over and end up walking the seemingly easier road. I say "easier" because fear is a natural response to unknown situations. It is much more difficult to practice the presence of God and live by faith than to simply give in to fear and take the path of least resistance. Hebrews 11:1 says this about faith: **"Now faith is being sure of what we hope for and certain of what we do not see."** When God gives us promises, it is because He intends to honor them. He cannot lie (Num.23:19), He must tell the truth and the truth is that He will **"never leave us or forsake us"** (Heb.13:5).

I am a very careful person; it is not in my nature to jump off of the diving board without first measuring how deep the water is in the pool below. Over the years God has asked me to trust Him and take many leaps of faith into the pool of life. He has never let me down, not even once. There has always been water in the pool and I have never smashed my face on the bottom – although it seemed like I would do precisely that most of the time. There did not always appear to be enough water to dive into, but there always was!

When God calls you to do something, He will provide for every need that you will face.

There have been times when I was expecting God to do

something a certain way, but what I expected to happen did not happen. Nevertheless, God has shown His faithfulness to me over the last twenty-seven years. It's His Kingdom, after all, and He runs it the way that He chooses. I must get in line with what He is doing; He is not motivated into action by what I think is best.

I have been through a very awesome but very difficult time in the last few years. I have had to face many of my fears, and couldn't run away from them anymore. I couldn't hide behind my leadership position to get out of facing up to some areas that needed to change in my life. Here are a few of the many fears that I faced and how the Lord has met me.

Will people like me when they find out what I'm really like?

First, I was afraid to let people know who I really was. I could not let anyone get close enough to see what I was like, except for my precious wife. Since I allowed this fear to control my life, I wouldn't let people get close to me, and I was forced to pretend to be someone that I was not. I had to face this lie head on, and when I did it turned out that it wasn't as scary as I thought it would be.

This is one of the most basic fears that everyone faces. I think that if people are true to themselves they will have faced this fear at one time or another. Some people just become very busy and don't allow themselves to ponder life questions.

I felt like I was the worst Dad in the world and that my children were all going to need therapy sooner or later. My friends responded by informing me that I was just like them: I didn't have the corner on losing my temper with my children. I was no worse or no better than other parents. Nothing that I did was outside of the grace of God, so I might as well just be myself and stop worrying. I was simply the person God had made me to be, and that had to be good enough. (I am talking about everyday life here and not parental abuse issues)

What you see is what you get; there isn't anything more – no tricks up my sleeve – and if God didn't come through and rescue me I wouldn't make it. Just think how good God is! He knows exactly what I'm like and He still loves me. When you think about it, aren't we all a little dysfunctional at times?

I needed to change my behavior in these situations I've mentioned and God used my friends to help me see that. As I stopped hiding and let people into my life, I was able to face up to my first fear. I realized that God still loved me even when I was grumpy and not that nice to be around. This truth meant so much to me: God the Father knew exactly what I was like and He still wanted to be my friend. This truth takes the pressure off of me to perform in an attempt to make everyone like me. I don't have to project a false image anymore; how good is that?

The second fear that I've faced is that somehow I was going to miss out on the path that God had for me in my life. I obviously didn't have enough faith in God to experience His goodness, faithfulness and guidance. I felt at times that I had made a horrible decision, and that I had surely stopped the flow of His blessings for my family. There were so many lies governing my life that it was hard for me to trust a loving God. I thank God he has allowed me to work through these issues!

There were many times when I felt completely lost and blind unable to see the path that was before me. I woke up early one morning feeling completely blind and God gave me this scripture from Isaiah 42:16:

"I will lead the blind by ways that they have not known, along unfamiliar paths I will guide them; I will turn the darkness into light before them and make the rough places smooth. These are the things I will do; I will not forsake them."

I took this as a personal promise from the Father's heart that he was going to lead me each step of the way. The truth was that, figuratively speaking, He took away my sight for awhile to teach me to follow Him. I now try to follow God by the truth laid out in scripture (2 Cor. 5:7) and not just by my mind, emotions, and will.

How do I follow someone that I cannot see? Take a look at

God's track record and see that He is completely faithful to the promises that He gives in scripture. The road of faith and trust is not easy to walk on, yet I know too much to go back to my old ways of fear and lies. Is God trustworthy? Of course He is! He says He will never leave me nor forsake me. The next question is; will **I** trust Him?

Brennan Manning has written an excellent book entitled *Ruthless Trust*. I would recommend that everyone read this book. Here is one thing that Brennan has to say about trust.

> *The basic idea is in one sentence: The splendor of a human heart that trusts and is loved unconditionally gives God more pleasure than Westminster Cathedral, the Sistine Chapel, Beethoven's Ninth Symphony, Van Gogh's Sunflowers, the sight of 10,000 butterflies in flight, or the scent of a million orchids in bloom. Trust is our gift back to God, and he finds it so enchanting that Jesus died for love of it.* [1]

Here is a real-life story illustrating of the scripture about the blind being led by God. I was at a well-attended church meeting in Abbotsford and was waiting outside in the lineup to go in. As I was standing there, I was pushed from behind. I don't like it when people are impatient, it really bothers me. I began thinking, "Since there's nowhere to go, why do you have to get pushy?" I decided that I should look behind me and see who was doing the pushing. To my astonishment there was a lady with dark sunglasses holding a white cane. God certainly had my attention at this point.

God started to speak to me in my heart. I thought that it was very significant that this blind person was there just after God had given me the above scripture from Isaiah. God is very practical and will use many different methods to teach us. This thought came to me as I was standing in the line-up: "Did you notice that she needed to have her friend guide her?"

All I could say was, "Yes, Lord." Another thought came to me; "Brian, did you notice that she wasn't fighting the person who was guiding her?" I was beginning to get the point. I had made my life more difficult by fighting God.

I came to the simple realization that God knows me and He promised that He will guide me even when I feel like I'm blind. I can rest in His wisdom and love and let Him take care of me. When anxiety starts to build about what is happening in my life I can go back to this scripture from Isaiah and depend on it for comfort and strength. I still struggle with anxiety but I am in process.

The third fear I have face is the fear of death. Over the years I have been through many things that threatened to derail my faith. In 1992 I was a program director at a Christian camp. A fifteen year-old girl was killed the last week of the summer. It was a very difficult experience that I never quite got over. Grief is a strange thing; it can come back for a visit at any time. I will never forget that summer. How could a loving God let something like this happen? I should have been there to protect her and keep her safe. She was such a sweet girl. *Why would this happen to her?*

The accident occurred on an overnight camp out, so we were out in the bush at the time. After the accident happened we had to gather the campers together who were in her cabin group and talk with them. I remember praying with the kids that God would have mercy and heal her. All God said to me was, **"Will you trust Me?"** I was completely numb at that point and had nothing to say. I didn't tell the campers; I just kept it to myself.

I had to do her memorial service at the camp the next day. I felt so awful, it was almost beyond my comprehension that God could allow something like this to happen. After I was finished the service, all I could do was lie on the floor and sob. God spoke to my heart with a very simple truth: **"My ways are not your ways. Let her go. It's her time."** God's mercy seems quite severe at times. Just the same, I realized that I had to pull myself together to try and bring comfort and truth to a bunch of hurting teenagers.

I could have easily pressured each camper into making a decision for Christ at that point. God made it very clear to me that I was not to use fear, guilt or manipulation to pull on people's heart strings to become Christians. Instead, we listened to the campers and did lots of sharing with each other. It was terribly hard, but God brought us all through.

A few summers back I was asked once again to direct a teen camp. I never realized how much fear was still in my heart towards teens and camp. I knew that God wanted me to face up to these fears and replace them with peace. During my first meeting with the camp director I turned about as white as a sheet. I was taken right back to 1992 and felt like something horrible was going to happen. It was about all I could do to keep going and organize the camp. I had a choice to make: was I going to live in fear or in faith?

I faced my fear about having another camper dying at the camp. There was no other way through that situation. I trusted the Lord with the safety of the campers and did everything I could to ensure their safety. Nothing of any consequence happened and I realized that most of the things that I fear will never come to pass. I needed to face life as it happens and not as it *could* happen. (See Matt. 6:34.)

A Simple Object Lesson

Let me introduce you to one of my friends and Elders. Bill Pegg has meant a lot to me over these last years; he is a man of God and has walked with me through many trials. Bill spent many years out of the limelight, serving God quietly, running a small business and raising his family. Bill and his dear wife Jamie joined us when we planted Freshwind Christian Fellowship. They were a precious gift from the heart of God, true servants that were not afraid to jump in and get involved. They took on the kids program, which was a huge help to us.

Bill hears from God. He has valued the voice of God in his life and as a result he hears God often. God made it clear to Bill that if He opened a door of opportunity Bill was to walk through it no matter how much fear he felt. Bill is the real deal, no cardboard cutout Christian here. He has walked through these doors many times and has grown as a result. He has never attended Bible College; his schooling for leadership came through years of living life and making good, godly decisions.

It became obvious to the leadership of Freshwind Christian Fellowship that Bill and Jamie were to join the leadership team as elders. And what do elders do? Elders eld, and that's what Bill and Jamie were doing. They were caring for the flock and we felt God was calling them to leadership. They joined us and stepped through the open door of opportunity even though it was scary for both of them – but they wouldn't let fear stand in the way of what God had for them.

After a few years, the leadership team sensed a strong leading to invite Bill to come on staff with Freshwind CF; this was another door that God was opening before Bill. He stepped through the door and has not looked back. Who knows what God has for Bill and Jamie in the future? I don't know, but I am confident that God will see them through whatever comes their way.

Bill has helped me to face fear issues in my own life. He raised three sons of his own and has experienced all the resultant joys and trials. There is no replacement for years of experience, which is why the title of "elder" fits him so well. I remember one particular day when I was struggling with my relationship with my kids; Bill was there to confront me on my attitude. He helped me to see that I was trying to control them so that they would act the way I wanted them to. He pointed out that if I continued to act this way I would drive a wedge in between us, which was the last thing I wanted to do. I listened to Bill's wise words and stepped away from this behavior. I still struggle with these issues, but my kids and I are getting along pretty well these days.

I was involved in youth work for many years. I used to think I was pretty cool; I had all the answers for parents that were struggling with their children. If those parents would only be cool like me then their kids would respect them and they would get along with each other. (Just how arrogant can a person be anyway?) Then I had teenagers of my own. There is a huge difference between being a youth worker and being a parent. My kids did *not* think that I was cool at all and they did not like to be around me sometimes – and this hurt deeply. I suddenly had lots of empathy for parents. Parenting really is one of the hardest jobs that there is. We're not given any sort of manual, yet we're expected to be experts at it.

I chose to trust the Lord with my kids and pray for them every day, rather than respond to them in fear and mistrust. God has given us three of the most awesome kids on the face of the earth, but they're normal and need to be understood rather than preached at. To be honest I'm much better at telling them what they need to do rather than taking the time to listen to what they have to say, but I'm learning.

I choose to face my fears about my children today; they are God's kids and not mine. They have been on loan from God and need to be free to go back to Him as they grow and mature. Walking along the road called faith is not for the fainthearted; it takes courage and perseverance. I choose to face the fears I have about the future and about what is going to happen in my life. I choose to place my past, present, and future in His very capable hands and try and live from faith rather than fear.

Endnotes

1   The Dick Staub Interview: Brennan Manning on Ruthless Trust –Christianity Today Web Site -Posted 12/10/2002

8

LIFE AS A MARATHON

The Tortoise and the Hare

The hare was once boasting of his speed before other animals. "I have never yet been beaten," said he, "when I put forth my full speed. I challenge anyone here to race with me." The Tortoise said quietly, "I accept your challenge." "That is a good joke," said the hare. "I could dance around you all the way." "Keep boasting until you've beaten me," answered the tortoise. "Shall we race?"

So a course was fixed and a start was made. The hare darted almost out of sight at once, but soon stopped and, to show his contempt for the tortoise, lay down to have a nap. The tortoise plodded on, and plodded on, and when the hare awoke from his nap, he saw the tortoise nearing the finish line and he could not catch up in time to save the race.

Plodding wins the race. [1]

I can identify with both the Tortoise and the Hare in Aesop's fable. I used to think that life was like a hundred-yard dash. Run as fast and hard as you can, do everything you can to save the world. Then I turned forty and crashed physically and emotionally. I crashed so hard that there was very little left of me to even *think* about running a hundred-yard dash. I came to realize through my recovery process that life is more like a marathon race. Some people say that they would rather "burn out than rust out." I would guess that these people haven't been through a burnout themselves.

Slow and steady is the best way to run a marathon; marathoners need to learn this if they are to finish the race. After all it's great to start the race, but it's better to finish the race and receive the prize at the end. There may be energy to begin the race, but you don't receive a prize for a perfect start.

I have become a plodder; I try to just keep putting one foot in front of the other and keep walking. I used to be quite good at sprinting. I could run those hundred yards very efficiently and effortlessly. I never realized that God was not in a hurry and that He did not need me to run so fast. **I thought that I understood God and His ways, but I was sadly mistaken.**

I was involved in various aspects of youth work for almost fifteen years. I thought that the nature of youth work was somewhat of a hundred-yard dash: I only had these young people for a short time, so I had to run hard and run fast to keep up with them and be relevant to them. I didn't understand that they needed role models of long-term real Christianity lived out in everyday life. These young people needed fathers and mothers, not super-cool youth workers. I used to have all the answers that young people needed to hear, I could relate to them and their problems. I didn't know that I was supposed to train them to prepare to run their own marathon races. I probably passed on the hundred-yard dash mentality to the young people I was trying to help mature.

I have never actually run a marathon, but I know several people that have. There is arduous training involved in order to complete a marathon; one doesn't go out and run a marathon on a whim, although there are exceptions to every rule. Imagine running twenty-six point two miles? That's long way, even for people who are super-fit! Training often starts months in advance, stamina needs to be built up for the task ahead. The distance the person runs is increased as each week goes by so that by the time of the marathon race the runner is ready for the distance.

There are a lot of similarities between running a marathon and the Christian life: both require character, perseverance, correct methods of training, healthy eating habits, and a good amount of sleep (rest) before and after the race. Marathon runners must learn to pace themselves if they are to finish the race. Even with all these things taken into account there is still the "wall" that the marathoner will face at about twenty miles into the race. The wall is when the body runs out of nutrients to burn and starts to shut down. It then takes sheer willpower to finish the race, which is very similar to the Christian life!

How many Christian leaders have we seen taken out of the race because they made very bad choices when faced with the "wall" of difficulties in their own lives? That's why it's so important that leaders have been tested and tried in the furnace of affliction. It's not fun, but this testing is crucial. The Bible instructs us to make sure that the leaders we put in place are not new Christians; they need to have maturity to run the race. They need to have proven character, to keep going when life gets tough. (See 1 Tim. 3:1-10.)

The journey is just as important as the destination!

Thank God for the journey that He takes us on every day! In order to enjoy this journey we need to live today, be present in this moment. Sometimes it's easier to live in tomorrow or yesterday, and then we don't have to face up to today. What does it mean to be present? One of the meanings is that we live in the here and now. I encourage you to read *Ruthless Trust* by Brennan Manning. He talks about living in the present.

"The real value of Ruthless Trust is found in the chapter entitled, "The Geography of Nowhere." Trusting God allows ragamuffins to live in the "now" and "here". (Manning's nowhere) Unfettered by the guilt of the past or anxiety for the future; ragamuffins live fully in the present. (The present is the only place where God can be experienced.)[2]

When we live in the past we don't have to face the present. We say to ourselves that life was so good back then. How can we ever get back there again? Or we become paralyzed living in the land of regrets, thinking about what we should have done.

When we live in the future we can look forward to things with anticipation in our hearts. Life will be so good when this or that happens, we will be very happy then. The only problem with this is that we still have to deal with all of our issues when we arrive at this future destination. We can never escape the truth of who we really are; we just get good at pretending. "If you don't deal with your past it will deal with you."

We have to face the truth about ourselves: we can't do life on our own, and we need God. As we face these facts, God comes close and wraps His arms around us. He speaks tenderly to us and gives us His Holy Spirit that helps us change and become more like Jesus. We cannot live vicariously through anyone else; we have to walk on the path that He has set out for us. Yet God is always with us and is not ashamed of us, He'll never turn His back on us. We are accepted for whom we are, but He loves us too much to let us stay they way we are.

I used to be a destination person, a forward-looking visionary! I lived this way for so long that I didn't have to face up to the pain I was feeling at the present moment. There was no joy in the journey for me. I actually disassociated for as long as I can remember. Disassociation has become an epidemic in society today, and this turning away from life and creating a false realty is easier to deal with than the present situation.

I didn't want to face up to my daily life so I would turn away. I don't blame anyone for living this way. It's one way to deal with the trauma that we have experienced in the past. However, I would like to suggest that there is a better way of dealing with life than running away when things get difficult; we need to face up to whatever comes our way. We need to turn towards the Lord instead of running away and hiding from Him. We need to learn to find a place to stand in the midst of the trials that we are facing.

Marathon runners need to face the pain they are feeling in order to deal with it and finish the race. How can we face life rather than turning away and hiding?

I am now starting to find joy in the midst of everyday life. I still struggle with living in the future, but it's a lot different now. I don't think I have that faraway look in my eyes near as much anymore. Being present and accountable is a very important thing. As we live in the present moment, we can experience the real joys and sorrows of life. We actually get to live our lives rather than letting life pass us by.

If life is more like a marathon, then I need to slow down and "smell the roses along the way." I do this in many different ways now. My work week has changed drastically from what it used to be like. I am far more intentional now; I try not to let the tyranny of the immediate dictate my schedule anymore. I am learning to respond to people with needs around as Jesus leads me to respond. Someone once told me that a need does not necessarily constitute a call.

Jesus said that He only did what He saw the Father doing. He lived to please His Father in Heaven (See Jn 5:19; 8:29.) Jesus made time for contemplation each day, a time set aside to be quiet and reflective, taking time to talk with His Father.. I can only give away in public the things that I have received in private from God. I don't want to give the impression that I'm a spiritual giant and have everything in perspective; I just know that contemplation is important for everyday life.

Getting regular exercise has become part of my work week as well. I try to go to the gym on a regular basis, staying in shape is important to me. Physical activity affects how we deal with stress as well. I realized a number of years ago that I could benefit by walking each day. Walking helps me clear my head and reflect upon the important things in life. Walking is a great prescription for stress. There have been so many times when I have been stressed out and I realize that I need to go out for a walk. The stress melts away like butter on a freshly-cooked cob of corn.

I can talk to God as I walk, which some people have called **prayer walks**. I walk and I talk. I get the issues stressing me out and off of my chest. Walking has become a very important part of my day. I also take time to reflect on nature as I walk, learning to appreciate how God has made our world. I am learning to be contemplative, taking time to appreciate the things that God appreciates.

> **"This is what the LORD says: "Stand at the crossroads and look; ask for the ancient paths, ask where the good way is, and walk in it, and you will find rest for your souls. But you said, 'We will not walk in it.'"** (Josh 6:16)

There are so many "good" things that take away this time of quietness before God. As a matter of fact, I would rather be going full tilt and keep myself busy; then I don't have to take the time to be quiet. We are instructed from Isaiah 40:31 to "wait on the Lord and we shall renew our strength." This waiting is not just sitting around watching the world go by. Waiting on the Lord is seeking His wisdom and heart about our lives. Waiting is an active word, as opposed to being a couch potato in front of the TV.

Marathoners need to be completely focused on the task at hand. They can't be concerned about how their investments are doing while they're running. They can't let the cares and concerns of the world take their attention away from the race. It's the same for us as Christians: we can't let our attention be drawn away from the important things in life.

This theme reminds me of my dear friend and mentor, Eric McCooeye. Eric and I have been in relationship for a long time. He had a tremendous impact on my life; he has been a father to me for many years. Eric spoke an important statement into my life which I have never forgotten.

The setting was a church service and I had asked him to consider being a prayer supporter for me and my family. Eric has learned the secrets of running this marathon called life; it's all about learning to live from in an attitude of peace and rest rather than living in striving and stress. When I asked Eric about praying for my family he said that He had to pray about it. That answer impacted me; he was not just jumping into a commitment to pray for us on a regular basis without first asking permission from God. That is also a very important principle. Then he looked me straight in the eyes and spoke this word into my heart: "The cares and concerns of the world are choking out the first place that God wants in your life."[3]

I had a choice to make at that point. I could disagree with him and try and argue my way out of listening to him, or I could agree with him and learn to become a man of God. I had been letting "life" take the place of God. I have struggled with worrying ever since I was born. I have a hard time relaxing and letting go. Look at what Jesus spoke to His disciples in Matthew 6:

> **"Therefore I tell you, do not worry about your life, what you will eat or drink; or about your body, what you will wear. Is not life more important than food, and the body more important than clothes? Look at the birds of the air; they do not sow or reap or store away in barns, and yet your heavenly Father feeds them. Are you not much more valuable than they? Who of you by worrying can add a single hour to his life? And why do you worry about clothes? See how the lilies of the field grow. They do not labor or spin. Yet I tell you that not even Solomon in all his splendor was dressed like one of these. If that is how God clothes the grass of the field, which is here today and tomorrow is thrown into the fire, will he not much more clothe you, O you of little faith? So**

do not worry, saying, 'What shall we eat?' or 'What shall we drink?' or 'What shall we wear?' For the pagans run after all these things, and your heavenly Father knows that you need them. But seek first his kingdom and his righteousness, and all these things will be given to you as well. Therefore do not worry about tomorrow, for tomorrow will worry about it- self. Each day has enough trouble of its own" (Mat. 6:25-34).

This was one of those times when God's word came and laid me bare. This passage in Matthew is one of my favorites in the entire Bible. There is nothing I can gain from worrying, except an ulcer perhaps. I know these things in my head, but I am still learning them in my heart. As Heidi Baker said, we need a "smaller brain and a bigger heart." Our brains get in our way at times; they need to be brought under the authority of Jesus Christ and line up with His truth from the Bible.

Marathon runners need to realize that a slow and steady pace will get them to the finish line. They may not come in first place but they are going to finish the race and receive the prize that waits them at the end. Just completing the race is enough of a reward after running twenty-six miles.

In life, the important question is not if you started well, but did you finish well? As the old saying goes, "the road to hell is paved with good intentions."[4] Life is not lived well in the fast lane; it is to be lived one moment at a time. We need to slow down and experience each day as it comes. Hundred-yard dash runners don't see anything but a blur as they run their race. Slow and steady may not be very exciting but it's a great way to become a marathon runner in the race called life.

Endnotes

1   Aesop's Fables
2   Book Review of Ruthless Trust - www.wineskins.org
3   From the various sayings of Eric McCooeye
4   St. Bernard of Clairvaux, 1150 AD

9

SUFFERING IS NOT AN OPTION

The world is full of suffering, it is also full of overcoming it. **(Helen Keller)**[1]

Let me say right from the start that I am not an expert in suffering; I just want to explore this subject. Suffering is not an option; it's not something that we can choose to avoid. There are a few things that human beings have in common, and suffering is one of them. Life is rarely as neat and as tidy we would like; we will all face storms of one kind or another. Yet, as we live together in community, we have an opportunity to enter into each other's experience of suffering. We are called as Christians to "love our neighbors as ourselves." There are countless ways that this can be done; one of the ways is by being there for people who are having a hard time, to "mourn with those who mourn" (Rom. 12:15) and to encourage the discouraged (Isa. 35:3-4).

I am writing this chapter for a number of reasons; I want to talk about real-life issues that matter to all of us. Suffering is such a natural part of life, but I don't see a good theology of suffering in many churches today. I believe that there can be redemptive purposes and important lessons to be learned even in the midst of suffering. I believe that, as we learn to embrace suffering, we will become more compassionate and human in the process. I am a fellow sufferer looking for answers that make sense.

- *If God so loves, why did He allow these awful things to happen?*
- *What good can come from suffering?*
- *Where is God when it hurts?*
- *Why does He seem to take people before their time?*
- *Why doesn't God heal everybody all the time?*

Have you ever asked these kinds of questions? You are not alone, because everybody feels like this at one time or another. There are many different ways to respond to suffering. It's in our human nature to ask questions and to try and find meaning in the midst of life, but there are times when there does not seem to be an answer. One person will get angry, while another will not want to face the truth of what is happening. I don't blame anyone for responding in either of these ways; I've done it myself. Life can be so hard at times that it seems like someone is playing a cruel joke on us. Pretending that everything is fine is one option for dealing with our everyday reality, but it doesn't do us any good in the long run.

"I do not believe that sheer suffering teaches. If suffering alone taught, all the world would be wise, since everyone suffers. To suffering must be added mourning, understanding, patience, love, openness, and the willingness to remain vulnerable." [2]

I have come to a couple of conclusions about a stubborn fact of life: everyone will experience suffering in one way or another, and there are times when it seems there are no answers to bring comfort to the person who is suffering. Christians are not exempt from suffering in life. (See 2Tim 3:10-12) There is no prayer that will keep trouble away; it's a normal part of life. I have learned that I don't have to answer every question that is asked of me when people ask why God allows suffering, but I *do* need to learn to enter into people's lives and suffer with them.

Christian spirituality is not a silver bullet that will protect us from the trials of life.

While there are countless promises found in the bible, *none* of them give us a way of *escaping* suffering. The Bible treats suffering as a fact, not as a "theory". The Bible speaks of WHEN we suffer, not IF we suffer. There are some theological traditions that believe that all suffering is evil and that God would never allow difficult situations to occur or hard things to happen in the believer's life. The longer I live, the more I see that this theology is based on what **should be**, rather than on **what is**. I wish that I never had to face hard things, and that my life was one long sunny day, but, as we all know, that's not the way of things in this world. The important thing is not the fact of suffering, but that we can find **meaning** and **hope** in the midst of tragedy and hardships.

"When the crisis you're facing makes you want to throw in the towel, remember this: our problems become God's opportunities. He loves to transform our most costly mistakes into priceless gems of wisdom, our bruised and bleeding places into greater strength, and our deepest fears into unshakable faith..."[3]

How in the world can we rejoice in our suffering?

"Not only so, but we also rejoice in our sufferings, because we know that suffering produces perseverance; perseverance, character; and character hope. And hope does not disappoint us, because God has poured out his love into our hearts by the Holy Spirit whom He has given us" (Rom. 5:3-5).

The only way that we can rejoice in our suffering is by keeping our eyes firmly fixed on the Lord Jesus Christ. He is our role model for living. When He walked on the earth, his perspective was that life was more than the here and now. His perspective was eternal. He knew who He was and where He was going. Jesus also knew that suffering could produce good fruit in His life. What happened to Jesus as a result of His perfect obedience? Being obedient cost Jesus His life. What does that tell you about our lives if we follow Jesus? It is not easy to live as a real biblical Christian in today's world. Can we expect any other sort of path than what our Shepherd walked on?

> **"During the days of Jesus' life on earth, he offered up prayers and petitions with loud cries and tears to the one that could save him from death and He was heard because of His reverent submission. Although He was a son, he learned obedience from what He suffered and, once made perfect, he became the source of eternal salvation for all who obey Him…"**
> (Heb. 5:7-8)

Jesus learned to obey His Father through what He suffered. Does that give you a clue as to what we may experience in our lives? What does that tell you about the times that we suffer? Character is developed through hard times; lessons can be learned through trials.

You can't have God's power without experiencing His suffering!

I'm basically a wimp. I don't like this path that Jesus laid out for me, but there's no *other* way to live life. I would rather experience the "power of His resurrection" than the "fellowship of sharing in his sufferings" (Phi. 3:10). But we can't have His power without joining in His suffering; we wouldn't appreciate what God has given us if we just experienced His power. Operating in God's power is wonderful, but it doesn't necessarily develop character; that is developed through being obedient even in the midst of suffering and trials. Character is developed in the storms of life, not when everything is sunny and pleasant.

I want to follow Jesus with all of my heart, but I don't want to suffer. I don't go out and look for ways to suffer. But who really knows what each day will bring in our lives? Am I going to have a better reward in heaven because of all of the hard things that I had to endure? I'm not sure about that, but I do know that I'm still going to serve God and love His people, regardless of personal gain (at least it sounds good on paper).

God will not allow us to walk in his miraculous power until we have His heart. That way, we won't try and use His power for our own advancement or selfish gain. We acquire the heart of God through times of suffering as we make good choices to learn and grow through them. Otherwise, if we haven't been tested in the furnace of affliction, we may be tempted to run when the going gets hard.

Suffering is a natural by-product of being obedient to Jesus. He suffered and we will as well. Everyone suffers at one time or another; it's one of the few things that all humans have in common. What form will suffering take in our lives today?

> "Friends, when life gets really difficult, don't jump to the conclusion that God isn't on the job. Instead, be glad that you are in the very thick of what Christ experienced. This is a spiritual refining process, with glory just around the corner." (1Pet. 4:12, 13 The Message)

We are not called to walk by fear but are called to walk by faith. We are to embrace life with all that we are, even though we will inevitably face suffering. Imagine talking to people from New Orleans just after Hurricane Katrina hit. They would have some wisdom about suffering that they did not have before the hurricane hit.

What are you facing today? Perhaps you have been denied that job promotion because you wouldn't budge from your convictions. You might feel like God has forgotten you, put you on some shelf to live out your life by yourself. You could actually be going through physical persecution for your faith and wonder what you did to deserve this treatment. The only thing that you did was follow Jesus, and look where that got you. You may be facing a terminal disease right now. The doctors may have pronounced a death sentence in your life, but don't give up; God may have other things in store for you.

Welcome to the school of pain. There are not that many

who are willing to continue on in this school; the tuition almost kills you!

I have heard a lot of trite sayings since I became a Christian. Some of them make me a little queasy, but lots of them are true. When you face various trials and struggles you can become "bitter or better" through the experience. Every single day there are opportunities to make choices. Are you going to let your circumstances get the best of you, or are you going to trust God no matter what happens? I didn't say that it was going to be easy, but it can be very rewarding.

Suffering has become a lot more than an intellectual exercise!

Suffering has become a lot more than just an intellectual exercise for me. I have faced my fair share of trials and have just gone through a bout with kidney stones. It's incredible how much pain one little stone can cause when it's being passed from your kidney to the outside world. Other than a few urinary tract infections, I had no early warning signs that I even had a kidney stone. My doctor decided that I needed to go see a specialist in order to track down the cause of the infections, which is when the "fun" began. (If you get queasy easily, skip over this section. I have a real life and I experience real pain.)

God designed every body part to have a certain function,

except perhaps for our appendix, but that is another subject altogether. Nevertheless, I needed to have all the normal guy tests that are given to ascertain what was wrong with my urinary tract. I am well past the age of forty and these tests have become a part of normal life.

If you're a guy and *your* Doctor ever mentions that you need to have a "cystoscopy," you may want to leave his presence very quickly. If you stay, prepare yourself for an interesting experience! I won't go into detail about this test; you can research it for yourself if you're so inclined. Suffice it to say that it hurt and the pain lasted a number of days. The scope gives the Doctor the ability to have a "wee peek" at what is happening inside you. Of course, there is only one way to get the scope into your bladder and that is where the pain part comes in.

I did not want this test and if there were any way to *avoid* it, I would've done so. I tried denying it but that didn't work very well, so I went through with the "procedure." I felt like a slab of beef sitting on the operating table, exposed to all who were within visual range. The nurse advised me that the freezing would be *a little cold;* this was the least of my worries. My manhood was "out there" and I felt rather out of my comfort zone. The nurses were reassuring, however, and helped to calm my well-founded fears. I was told that the cystoscopy would be very painful but would be over quickly.

This information was very important to help me fix my attention on the task at hand. I was very fortunate indeed that my urologist was such a talented guy. The cystoscopy was over before I knew it, and there was great rejoicing heard down the halls of the hospital. My doctor informed me that everything looked normal, although I had a slightly enlarged prostate.

The next test that I was to take was an ultrasound of my abdomen to determine, among other things, kidney function. After having the cystoscopy, the ultrasound was like a holiday to Hawaii in the month of January. The ultrasound exposed the kidney stone as a great huge rock, a centimeter in size. Although it was a "silent stone" (that means that I had no symptoms), it still had to be dealt with. I was sent to the Vancouver General Hospital to have the stone blasted by a machine called a "Lithotripter." This machine uses low and high frequency sound waves to blast kidney stones into little pieces that are easily passed out through the urine. Although the stone was silent for long time, it became quite vocal when introduced to the Lithotripter (which sounds and looks like something out of science fiction novel). The little bit had to come out. Unfortunately, these stones were not the right shapes to make them pass easily.

I woke up on Saturday morning at 3:00 am with the kind of pain that would make John Wayne cry like a baby. I paced the floor for about two and half hours. I couldn't get any relief from this pain, and nothing seemed to work. Finally I phoned my dear friend Eric and he told me to get to the hospital. I went there and they scolded me for not coming in right away. Since this was my first experience with kidney stone pain, I had no idea what to do. Within five minutes, my nurse had me hooked up to an IV filled with morphine that took my pain away. Actually, I could still feel the pain but it didn't really matter.

I didn't see it coming, and I wasn't prepared for the sort of pain that I went through. That sounds a lot like *life* to me. We are never prepared to suffer, but we must understand that this is going to happen. I was able to draw comfort from the fact that Jesus suffered a lot in His life; He is called "the suffering servant" at times. I was also able to endure the pain because I knew that I had friends out there praying for me and caring for me as I was in the hospital. I asked God to take this trial away from me but He said "no, He would take care of me every step of the way." There are things in life that I need to learn to *endure. It* does no good to curse God for the pain that I go through. When I curse God for all of my trouble, I end up living in the land of bitterness and anger.

I believe that God will take care of me no matter what I have to face. I have the power to choose to serve God and to not get bitter. The Bible does not give us empty promises that we will never go through tough stuff, it gives us healing promises that we can depend on.

> **"Consider it a sheer gift, friends, when tests and challenges come at you from all sides. You know that under pressure, your faith-life is forced into the open and shows its true colors. So don't try to get out of anything prematurely. Let it do its work so you become mature and well-developed, not deficient in any way"** (Jam. 1:2-4 The Message).

This Scripture is another one that I don't really like. Apparently God is not concerned about my likes and dislikes. **It seems that God is more concerned with my character than my comfort**. I must read this Scripture, take it to heart, and put it into practice in my life.

You may feel completely powerless today, yet you have the power to choose to do the right thing. Although good decisions can be hard to follow through, they produce a harvest of good fruit in our lives. Being honest is a good thing to do. Being kind to people when you don't have anything to gain is always the right thing to do. Helping people who are in need is also a good thing to do. As you make each good decision and follow through on it, you are building a strong foundation towards becoming mature. Choosing to be patient in the midst of suffering is a much better choice than becoming bitter and shriveling up in your spirit.

A Model to live by in the midst of suffering

"Praise be to the God and Father of our Lord Jesus Christ, the Father of compassion and the God of all comfort, who comforts us in all our troubles, so that we can comfort those in any trouble with the comfort we ourselves have received from God. For just as the sufferings of Christ flow over into our lives, so also through Christ our comfort overflows. If we are distressed, it is for your comfort and salvation; if we are comforted, it is for your comfort, which produces in you patient endurance of the same sufferings we suffer. And our hope for you is firm, because we know that just as you share in our sufferings, so also you share in our comfort.

"We do not want you to be uninformed, brothers, about the hardships we suffered in the province of Asia. We were under great pressure, far beyond our ability to endure, so that we despaired even of life. Indeed, in our hearts we felt the sentence of death. But this happened that we might not rely on ourselves but on God, who raises the dead. He has delivered us from such a deadly peril, and he will deliver us. On him we have set our hope that he will continue to deliver us, as you help us by your prayers. Then many will give thanks on our behalf for the gracious

**favor granted us in answer to the prayers of many"
(2 Cor. 1:3-11).**

The author of Second Corinthians was the Apostle Paul. He had more than his share of hardships. He suffered for his faith many times, but chose to keep trusting and serving God. He wrote to the believers at Corinth in order for them to understand about what was happening with him on his missionary journeys.

The above Scripture takes for granted the fact that we all have troubles and trials. Yet God the Father knows that we need Him to comfort us in our troubles. Paul calls God the "Father of compassion and the God of all comfort." God has compassion on His children; He loves us and is close to us when we are suffering.

One of the questions that people want answered is, "If God is so compassionate and kind, how can He let us suffer so much?" That is a valid question, but I'm not sure that there is one simple response that will give the kind of answer that people want. God was willing to send His Son to suffer and die on our behalf that we might choose to come into a relationship with Him. He knows suffering all too well. Jesus enters into our suffering and helps us through the difficult things that we are facing.

I have come to the conclusion that God is good whether I am doing well or doing poorly. It all depends upon how you choose to see life. What sort of outlook do you have on life? I know what it's like to have a negative outlook on life. I was very bitter for a long time. I have experienced the death of family and close friends, the times when nothing made sense. I have lived with pain for many years, I have asked God to heal me countless times, I have even had faith healers pray for me and yet I still live with this pain. Is there something wrong with me? Is there something I am missing? I am never going to stop asking God for healing. I will keep praying and believing, I can't base my faith on the fact that I am healed or not, I keep trusting that He's good.

I choose to believe what the writers of the Bible had to say about God and his character. I believe that God will be near to me and help me in all of my suffering. I have received comfort from knowing that God is close and will never leave me on my own. I have received comfort and help from being actively involved in Christian community. At the same time, I have also been able to comfort others in hard times with the comfort that I have received from God. The fact that I can comfort others with God's comfort is a miracle of grace from God. Suffering may be a fact of life but I'm going to continue to try and find meaning and hope in the midst of it. I leave you with this song written by William J & Gloria Gaither:

Because He (Jesus) lives, I can face tomorrow.

Because He lives, all fear is gone.

Because I know He holds the future,

And life is worth the living just because He lives.[4]

Endnotes

1   Helen Keller
2   Joseph Addison
3   *The Word for You Today* - December 21, 2005 – "Stay in Step With God" (3) Copyright 2005, Bob Gass Ministries.
4   Copyright 1971. Written by William J. Gaither and Gloria Gaither.

10

NOW THAT WE'RE DONE: ESSAYS FROM THE JOURNEY

I can't believe that I'm finally writing the conclusion to this book. When I started this project, I felt like a mountain climber with bad knees setting out to climb Mt Everest. There was no way that I could imagine actually finishing this book. Instead of allowing my paranoia to disable me, I just kept plodding along writing a little each day and before I knew it, this project was complete. There is a process to writing and it can be done.

One of my friends challenged me to try writing an hour a day and see what would happen. I figured that I could do that, but what would I write about? I chose to concentrate on some lessons I have learned along the way. I want to become a good writer which means that I have to keep writing. Some people may be born with the gift to write but I am not one of those. My editor was very kind to me, he said that I was not a professional writer but at least I had something to say.

Each of us must walk the path that Jesus has chosen for us. I can't live your life and you can't live mine, but there are some principles that are the same for everyone. I tried to write about some of these principles throughout the book. We don't get to push the easy button just because we follow Jesus and His teachings. We will experience life just like everyone else, but having a living relationship with God can help make sense of life and the troubles that come our way.

I set out in this book to talk about everyday people and everyday problems that come our way. I am a simple person and I wrote a simple book. Hopefully, your heart has been touched and encouraged by something that you have read. There are some who will say that this book is too simple or not theological enough; they are probably right, but I will not let critics hold me back from dreaming my dreams and seeing them come to fulfillment! Besides, dreaming is free so go ahead.

> *"It is not the critic who counts*; not the man who points out how the strong man stumbles, or where the doer of deeds could have done them better. *The credit belongs to the man who is actually in the arena*, whose face is marred by dust and sweat and blood, who strives valiantly; who errs and comes short again and again; because there is not effort without error and shortcomings; but who does actually strive to do the deed; who knows the great enthusiasm, the great devotion, who spends himself in a worthy cause, who at the best knows in the end the triumph of high achievement and who at the

worst, if he fails, at least he fails while daring greatly. *So that his place shall never be with those cold and timid souls who know neither victory nor defeat.* "[1]

I will leave you with this rather poignant story of how God has spoken to me lately, because I believe that it kind of sums up my life. My family and I have had the privilege of being involved in some amazing churches over the last couple of decades. I have seen some things happen in church to make me want to cry and laugh all at the same time. In the last few years we have been involved in helping churches going through transition. These times can be very stressful and sometimes feel rather uncomfortable. Sometimes transition feels like chaos, but I have come to understand that God is okay with a little chaos once in awhile. God also has a *process to work out in the midst of* transition or change, and we must trust that He knows what He's doing.

For the last year and a half we have been living in a small town in the Southern Okanagan called Summerland. It's always a lot easier to talk about taking a step of faith than actually taking that step. I spent the first year on part time staff at the Kelowna Gospel Mission, working in the "Men of Destiny" addictions recovery program. During this time I continued to be involved with Freshwind Ministry as I have done for the last decade. Currently I am working two days a week at Teen Challenge (www.bcteenchallenge.com) in

Winfield BC in a mentoring role with the staff and students.

Do I have what it takes? No, but I know who I need to follow and trust in this endeavor. Jesus knows exactly what needs to happen for these guys to recover and lead meaningful lives. God has called and is supplying in incredible ways. **"He always takes care of all of our needs and some of our wants."** I am very proud of these men that are trying to make changes and become who God originally wanted them to be. It's takes a lot of courage to face the truth, these guys are facing it day in and day out. Are they all going to make it? No. But does that mean that we should not give them an opportunity to try? I have learned more from the guys than they have learned from me: it has been an unforgettable course on perseverance and faith in the face of overwhelming discouragement.

God is not the God of second chances only: He is the God that keeps relentlessly pursuing a relationship with us even to our last breath. He never gives up on anyone and He never plays favorites, He loves everybody. No one is outside of the grace and mercy of God.

Does it ever seem to you that God is a million miles away and that He isn't responding to your cries for help? He has not forgotten about the promises that He made to you. He has everything under control. His love is never dependent on our behavior. It comes down to timing: when the time is right He will do what He said He would. He's seldom early but never late, which drives me crazy at times.

I sensed God speaking to me about all these blessings. He seemed to say to me: **"My blessings expose your heart and my heart at the same time. Brian, you really don't believe that I want to bless you and take care of you and your family, which is why you struggle with life so much. My heart is exposed for being generous and kind, I'm always that way. I love to take care of my children. Your heart is exposed and all the fear is out in the open. I love you and will never turn my back on you."** All I could do was to agree with Him and ask Him to heal my unbelief.

Is it easy to trust the process that God has for each one of us? No! Yet, I would never trade my life with anyone in a million years. We are going to continue to follow Jesus and see where He goes!

I trust that it was worth the time you spent reading this book. What has touched your heart from these "Essays from the Journey?" Perhaps you may want to take some time and write about these thoughts in your journal? I know that I am assuming that you all keep a journal, why not think about starting one if you don't already have one going? I have faith for you in your journey that you will meet God and experience His love and grace as you live your life. What's that? I hear you saying that you don't deserve to experience God or

His goodness, none of us do, it's just in His nature to pour out His blessings on His kids!

"For I know the plans I have for you," declares the LORD, "plans to prosper you and not to harm you, plans to give you hope and a future. 12 Then you will call upon me and come and pray to me, and I will listen to you. 13 You will seek me and find me when you seek me with all your heart. 14 I will be found by you," declares the LORD, "and will bring you back from captivity." (Jer. 29:11-14)

Endnotes

1   Theodore Roosevelt, *Man in the Arena"* Speech given April 23, 1910 : 26th president of US (1858 - 1919)

THANKS A BUNCH!

Now I understand the phrase, "books don't just happen."

How can I begin to say thank you to all the people that have made me what I am today? I am the product of a loving God, churches and ministries that have encouraged me over the years and built me up. Instead of giving up on me, my friends have stuck with me and weathered the hard times to help me get healed. For those who can remember, I was a little "rough around the edges" when I first started attending church. I am living proof that it's never time to give up and walk away from people who are hurting. There is no one outside of the grace of God.

There are a number of people that I would like to recognize in the writing, correcting and details of putting this book together. First of all, thanks to my sweet wife Sue. She believes in me and has stood with me for the last twenty-six years. What a women of faith! She puts up with a lot from me; I am not the easiest person to live with. Sue kept encouraging me and prodding me to write, so I did. Thanks to my three awesome kids as well, Jordan Ashley and Amanda, they have been an inspiration to me to keep going even when

I felt like quitting.

Here are a few others that I would like to mention: Ed Strauss (my editor) who was incredibly encouraging throughout the writing process. Thank you to Brad Haima of Circle Graphics who designed the cover for me. Brad and Eden Jersak, Ron Dart, Shelene Mitchell, Chad and Pam Tiegen all helped greatly with the writing, editing and proofreading of *Pilgrims Process*. Steve and Sylvia Schroeder also come to mind; they always keep me in line and give me great perspective. Steve ultimately came up with the title.

There are a number of other people that I would like to mention as well: Eric and Sally McCooeye, Ian and Janice Ross, Bill and Jamie Pegg, John and Erna Schmidt (I greatly miss you John), Steve and Cathy Dudgeon, Jim and Debbie Marten, Gary and Sherrine Cropley, Blayne and Betty Griener, Len and Debbie Wiens, Del Reimer, Andy and Jacquie Macpherson, Jason and Christine Goertzen, Cam and Michelle Stuart, Trevor Walters, Randy and Joan Rye, John and Carol Arnott, to name just a few. I know that I am missing lots of other people but they know who they are! ☺